Series

# Create Your Sales Network

*Practical guide for entrepreneurs, sales managers, area managers, and anyone who wants to build a successful sales force.*

## Massimo Marchetti

*All rights reserved*

*No part of this book may be reproduced, or stored in a retrieval system, or transmitted in any form or by any means, electronic, mechanical, photocopying, recording, or otherwise, without the express written permission of the publisher.*

*ISBN Code: 9798340303264*
*Publishing house: Independently published*

*Disclaimer:*
*The information in this guide is provided for informational and educational purposes. The author will not be held liable for any damages resulting from the use of this information. Users are encouraged to consult a professional for their specific business and legal needs.*

*First edition: September 2024*

# FOREWORD

Thank you for taking the time to devote to this guide, an integral part of the **latuaretedivendita.com** series that I hope will profitably accompany you in the creation and management of a modern sales network. My goal is to provide you with practical advice for creating and managing your network, which is why I prefer to call it a "guide," a term that reflects exactly what the topic requires.

Unlike many books that promise applicable suggestions but focus excessively on authors' personal stories, I have chosen a different approach. Drawing on 30 years of experience in the field and extensive study, I focused exclusively on content that can enrich you, the reader, without digressing into personal stories.

The guide is designed for those seeking practical understanding, those ready to experiment with new approaches, or those who want to delve deeper into the subject. It goes beyond theory, enriched with concrete examples and immediately applicable advice, including suggestions on software to integrate into your business, detailed scripts, and sample dialogues. In some cases, some concepts may be repeated in the various books in the series, sometimes just summarizing the salient points and sometimes going into more detail. This is not a distraction, but a definite choice to maintain consistency with the subject matter.

If you are a veteran in the field and find that these pages do not add anything new to your body of knowledge, I sincerely appreciate the time taken to read and hope that they will at least serve as inspiration or confirmation of your practices.

Conversely, if you are looking for inspiration or guidance to get started or improve, I am confident that you will find this text a valuable starting point.

I wish you fruitful and, above all, inspiring reading.

The Author

# General Index

1. **Structure and Organization** .................................................. **4**
   *The Salesman* .............................................................................. *4*
   *Commercial Director* ................................................................... *6*
   *Area Manager* .............................................................................. *9*
   *Sales Area Support* .................................................................... *12*
2. **Territorial Subdivision and Hierarchy** ............................... **14**
   *Territory Analysis* ...................................................................... *14*
   *Assignment of Territories* .......................................................... *16*
   *A More Effective Hierarchical Structure* .................................... *20*
3. **Selection of the Sales Network** ........................................... **23**
   *The Ideal Candidate* .................................................................. *24*
   *Candidate Search Strategies* ..................................................... *26*
   *Selection and Evaluation* ........................................................... *28*
4. **Onboarding** ............................................................................ **36**
   *Pre-Onboarding* ......................................................................... *36*
   *Active Involvement* .................................................................... *39*
5. **Training Pathways** ............................................................... **42**
   *Training Program Hypothesis* .................................................... *42*
   *Learning Techniques* ................................................................. *52*
6. **Goal Setting** ........................................................................... **57**
   *Context Analysis* ....................................................................... *57*
   *"Smart" goals* ............................................................................ *59*
   *Performance Monitoring* ........................................................... *63*
7. **Effective Communication** .................................................... **69**
   *Communication in the Daily* ..................................................... *70*
   *Communication in Education* ................................................... *71*
   *Updates and Newsletters* ........................................................... *78*
8. **Support Strategies** ............................................................... **81**
   *Continuing Education Programs* ............................................... *81*
   *Sales Resources and Marketing Materials* ................................. *86*
9. **Recognition and Incentives** ................................................. **91**
   *Public Recognition* .................................................................... *91*
   *Incentive Strategies* ................................................................... *94*
10. **Two-way Communication** ................................................... **96**
    *Freedom of Expression* ............................................................. *96*
    *Complaints and Negative Feedback* .......................................... *99*

# 1. Structure and Organization

Let's begin this journey together in the creation of a sales network, examining carefully and rigorously each of the roles within a sales organization; we will analyze not only the individual responsibilities, but also the interconnectedness between these roles and how they can be optimized for business success. We will learn about the various players involved in the results of a sales network, examining the critical issues and strengths of each role.

## THE SALESMAN

He is responsible for direct sales to customers, we can also say the beating heart of the sales network. Understanding products/services and the ability to convince customers are the keys to success in this role. The role of the salesperson within a sales network represents the very core of business success. This figure not only acts as a direct interface with customers, but also embodies the first point of contact with the image and value of the company itself. Let us now look in detail at his responsibilities and the crucial impact he has on the company's growth and reputation.

### KEY INTERFACE WITH THE CLIENT

The rep acts as an emblem of the company to customers. His ability to communicate effectively and engaging, understanding customer needs, and offering customized solutions is the lifeblood of sales success. Its interaction is not limited to a simple transaction, but represents an opportunity to create a lasting bond.

### IN-DEPTH KNOWLEDGE OF PRODUCTS/SERVICES
A thorough knowledge of the products or services offered by the company is of paramount importance. A well-informed salesperson not only answers customers' questions thoroughly, but also conveys confidence and authority, thus creating added value during the customer interaction.

### PERSUASIVE AND ARGUMENTATION SKILLS
The ability to persuade represents the crucial piece. It is not merely a matter of selling a product or service, but of convincing the customer that what is offered meets a real need of his or her. Presenting the benefits-not just the features-clearly and convincingly is critical to guiding the customer over the threshold of purchase.

### CUSTOMER AND SOLUTION ORIENTATION
A successful salesperson does not focus solely on the immediate transaction, but grasps the long-term value derived from customer satisfaction. He actively listens to the customer's needs and proposes solutions aimed at building strong and lasting relationships.

### ADAPTABILITY AND AGILITY
The sales landscape is constantly changing. A successful salesperson not only adapts to changes, but embraces them as opportunities. He or she is able to learn and adopt new approaches, tools and strategies to remain competitive in a dynamic marketplace. This principle holds true for both younger and more experienced salespeople, who can often be reluctant to change.

## Critical issues

### PERFORMANCE PRESSURE
The salesperson is often under constant pressure to meet and exceed sales goals.

This pressure can generate stress and negatively affect performance if not managed properly.

### WASTE MANAGEMENT
Dealing with rejection and objections from customers can be emotionally challenging. The ability to handle rejection and maintain a positive attitude is crucial to salesperson resilience.

### LOW READINESS FOR NOVELTY
The salesperson today must show willingness to be up-to-date on products/services, technologies, and industry trends.

### TIME MANAGEMENT
Balancing time management between acquiring new clients, maintaining existing relationships and day-to-day administration can be a challenge.

## Strengths

### INTRINSIC MOTIVATION
Personal motivation is a key strength. Intrinsically motivated salespeople find the drive to achieve goals even in the most complex situations.

### DETERMINATION AND RESILIENCE
Dealing with rejection is an integral part of sales work. Strong determination and resilience enable you to overcome challenges and continue to pursue goals.

### CUSTOMER AT THE CENTER
Successful salespeople always place the customer at the center. The ability to understand customers' needs and offer tailored solutions is one of their main strengths.

## COMMERCIAL DIRECTOR

The sales manager represents an apex figure within the company, with specific responsibilities not only in sales leadership, but also in marketing and, in some cases, logistics. In our context, we will focus primarily on his or her role within the sales network, where his or her support is critical in overseeing the performance and ensure alignment with goals defined in collaboration with ownership. This figure not only acts as a leader, but also performs a number of essential tasks that have a direct impact on the performance of the entire sales team. Let us now examine the essential skills for a sales manager.

## Strategic Leadership

### SALES TEAM MANAGEMENT
The sales manager is responsible for the management and development of the sales team. This includes selection of team members, initial and ongoing training, and individual performance management.

### ESTABLISHING GOALS
Setting clear and measurable goals is one of the Sales Manager's main responsibilities. These goals must be aligned with the company's strategic objectives and must be able to motivate and guide the team toward success.

### SUPPORT AND COACHING
Providing ongoing support and coaching to salespeople is critical. The sales manager, with his or her experience and background, provides guidance, advice, and resources to help the team overcome challenges with more effective strategies.

## Performance Supervision

### MONITORING
The sales manager constantly analyzes team performance, using key metrics to assess the effectiveness of strategies and identify areas for improvement.

### FEEDBACK AND CORRECTION
Based on performance analysis, provides regular feedback to the team to recognize successes and identify areas for development. Corrects strategies or provides new directions based on results.

## Leadership and Support

### INTERFUNCTIONAL COORDINATION AND SUPPORT
Collaborates with other departments such as marketing, product, and customer service to ensure that corporate strategy is integrated and consistent across all areas.

### MOTIVATION AND TEAM BUILDING
The Sales Manager knows how to create a positive, stimulating and motivating work environment with his or her employees. He or she promotes a sense of team ownership, common purpose, and encourages collaboration among all team members.

## Resource Management

### BUDGET MANAGEMENT
Manages the sales budget, allocating resources strategically to maximize the efficiency of sales activities.

### PLANNING AND OPERATIONAL PLANNING
The sales manager plans short- and long-term sales activities, coordinating strategies to achieve long-term results.

## Critical issues

### OVERLOAD OF RESPONSIBILITY AND HEAVY PRESSURE
The sales manager must manage multiple responsibilities and may be overworked. Team management, goal setting, performance analysis and other activities require time and constant effort.
The pressure to achieve goals can be stressful and affect the ability to make key decisions.

### INTERPERSONAL CONFLICTS
Managing a team means dealing with individual dynamics, managing conflicts and motivating people with different styles and personalities.

### BALANCING OF COMPETENCIES
Must balance their leadership and management skills with an understanding of sales dynamics and the specific needs of the team.

## Strengths

### Effective Leadership
A strong sales manager is distinguished by the ability to lead and motivate the team, establishing a clear vision and inspiring others to achieve goals.

### Coaching and Development Skills
Ongoing team support and development are key elements. A sales manager who can provide effective coaching improves the skills of team members.

### Performance Management
Ability to analyze and evaluate team performance, identifying areas for improvement and taking corrective action.

### Effective Communication
Being able to communicate clearly and persuasively with both the team and other departments is critical to success.

### Adaptability and Problem Solving
Be able to adapt to market changes, solve complex problems and make quick and effective decisions.

### Planning and Organization
Ability to plan long-term strategies, maintain focus on goals, and organize resources effectively.

# AREA MANAGER

The functions performed and skills required partly coincide with those of the sales manager with the exception that his role is more operational, and being confined to a more limited geographic region, of relatively less responsibility.

## Superintendence of the Area

### Land Management
The Area Manager is responsible for managing a specific geographic area. This includes allocating resources, setting goals, and implementing targeted strategies to maximize sales in that region.

### SALES ACCOUNT COORDINATION
Oversees Sales Accounts, agents, vendors or salespeople (indoor or outdoor) operating in assigned area, supporting them in defining strategies, identifying growth opportunities and optimizing team performance.

## Coordination of Sales Strategies

### SYNCHRONIZATION OF STRATEGIES
The area manager works synergistically with sales management to ensure that sales strategies are aligned with business objectives in his or her area.

### IMPLEMENTATION OF THE CORPORATE GUIDELINES
Ensures that corporate guidelines are understood and applied correctly in its context, adapting them as necessary to the specific needs of the area.

## Oversight of Regional Performance

### PERFORMANCE ANALYSIS AND MONITORING
Constantly assesses sales performance in the region, using key data and metrics to identify area-specific trends, opportunities, and challenges.

### REPORTS AND REPORTING
Communicates regularly to business management or other stakeholders [1] performance, adopted strategies, and growth prospects for the assigned area.

## Support and Staff Development

### TRAINING AND DEVELOPMENT
Provides support and training to salespeople working in the area, facilitating the development of their skills and providing guidelines to improve their performance.

---

1 *Stakeholders* *are individuals or groups with direct interest or influence in the outcomes of a project, organization or enterprise.*

### Resources and Operational Support
Ensures that the team has the resources it needs to do its work effectively, providing logistical and operational support as needed.

## Critical issues
### Pressure on Performance
The area manager is responsible for sales performance in the region. This pressure can create stress and tension in dealing with set goals, but with time and awareness of one's abilities, it can become a valuable ally in achieving one's goals.

### Communication and Coordination
Coordinating the entire team across geographic locations requires effective communication and careful management of group dynamics.

### Changes and Local Needs
Changes in the market and local needs require strong adaptability to situations that may arise and often quick decisions.

## Strengths
### Leadership and Strategic Vision
The Area Manager leads by setting examples of good behavior and always provides the team with clear strategic direction for the success of the region.

### Analytical and Decision Making Skills
It uses common data and metrics to analyze each employee's performance and, based on them, makes informed decisions aimed at continuous improvement and personal and professional growth of the team.

### People Management
Is able to manage and motivate a diverse team, inspiring them to achieve sales goals and providing support where needed. Knows how to communicate properly with top management to whom he or she must report.

### ADAPTABILITY AND PROBLEM SOLVING
It faces challenges with flexibility and identifies creative solutions to solve emerging problems in the different geographic areas it manages, always maintaining a global vision that fosters constant adaptation and evolution of the company.

### EFFECTIVE COMMUNICATION
It clearly communicates what the business goals are, inspires the team, and creates a collaborative and productive work environment.
Show appreciation for each contribution, valuing different skills and encouraging the exchange of ideas to innovate and grow together.

### STRATEGIC COORDINATION
Coordinates sales strategies to maximize sales potential and align regional activities with corporate objectives.

### MANAGEMENT COMPLEXITY
Managing an entire region requires a broad strategic vision and the ability to balance different responsibilities and activities, which can be extremely challenging.

# SALES AREA SUPPORT

## Sales Support Specialist
These professionals provide operational and administrative support to the sales team. They manage back-office activities, support sales processes, manage documentation, and assist salespeople in managing customers.

## Sales Training Expert
These professionals focus on training and skill development for salespeople. They design training programs, offer workshops, provide educational materials, and monitor progress to improve the team's sales skills.

## Marketing Specialists
The marketing team provides sales support through branding strategies, advertising campaigns, promotions, and creation of sales support materials, ensuring that the

corporate message is consistent and effectively communicated to the target audience.

## Sales or Business Analysts
These professionals are responsible for analyzing sales data to identify trends, patterns and opportunities in the market.
They provide detailed reports on sales performance, helping to guide strategic decisions.

## Customer Success Manager
This position focuses on managing relationships with existing customers. They strive to maintain customer satisfaction, understand their evolving needs, and ensure that customers are satisfied and continuously engaged.

## Technical Support/Product Specialists.
These professionals provide technical support to customers and vendors to answer product/service questions, solve problems, and provide detailed information on product features and usage.

> In this first chapter, we have seen that setting up a proper organization structure is the crucial first step in creating an effective sales network. Success depends on clearly defined roles and responsibilities, the ability to adapt to change, and the ability to handle critical issues such as performance pressure and customer rejection. Intrinsic motivation and strategic leadership are key elements in driving the team toward optimal results and building lasting relationships with customers.

# 2. Territorial Subdivision and Hierarchy

Conducting a detailed and fair analysis of markets for effective territory allocation is a fundamental process in sales management. This involves identifying market opportunities, allocating resources optimally, and defining strategies aimed at maximizing performance. Often, sales network managers do not give proper emphasis to this activity, treating it superficially. Instead, it is a crucial preliminary analytical work, the outcome of which requires periodic reviews to ensure the continued effectiveness of sales strategies.

## TERRITORY ANALYSIS

### Demographic and Socioeconomic Data

**POPULATION SEGMENTATION**
Identify and understand the demographic characteristics of potential customers in an area. For example, age, income, occupation, and other factors that influence purchasing decisions.

**SOCIOECONOMIC TRENDS**
Evaluate socioeconomic trends in the area, such as demographic changes, new residential areas, or industrial developments that could affect the demand for products/services.

# Supply and Demand Analysis

## DEMAND ANALYSIS
Assess existing demand for the product or service in the specific area. Seek to understand current and potential demand.

## COMPETITION
Examine the competition in the area, including the number and type of competitors, their market share and sales strategies employed.

# Searching for Opportunities

## IDENTIFICATION OF OPPORTUNITIES NOT TAKE ADVANTAGE OF
Find areas or market segments underserved or neglected by competitors and understand how the company can capitalize on these opportunities.

## FUTURE TRENDS
Examine future trends, such as the development of new industries, demographic or technological changes, that may affect demand in the area.

# Resource Allocation

## ALLOCATION OF PROPORTIONAL RESOURCES
Allocate resources based on, sales potential and identified opportunities. For example, areas with higher growth potential may require more investment in terms of personnel, marketing, etc. Other parameters to consider are the size of the areas and their road viability through isochronous maps[2].

# Customer Data Analysis

## DEMOGRAPHIC AND GEOGRAPHIC DATA
Segment customers by demographic factors such as age, income, education, and also by geographic location to

---

[2] *Isochronous maps* are graphical representations that show the areas that can be reached within a given time period from a specific point using a particular means of transportation (such as walking, driving, or public transportation). These maps are useful for a n a l y z i n g accessibility and spatial coverage in terms of travel time.

Better understand purchasing preferences and behaviors in various areas.

### PURCHASING BEHAVIORS
Examine purchasing patterns, preferences, purchase frequency, and purchase value to divide customers into segments based on their purchasing behaviors.

## Definition of Key Territories

### IDENTIFICATION OF AREAS OF GREATER OPPORTUNITY
Use customer data to identify key territories with high sales potential or high-value customers.

# ALLOCATION OF TERRITORIES

Effective allocation of territories is vital to maximizing sales performance and ensuring equitable and strategic market coverage. This process involves several key steps, starting from target setting to ongoing monitoring and adjustment of allocations.

## Assignment Goals
The primary objectives of territory allocation include:

### IMPROVE MARKET COVERAGE
Ensure that each geographical area receives adequate attention, avoiding overlapping or neglected areas.

### REDUCE INTERNAL CONFLICTS
Clearly define boundaries to prevent disputes between vendors and ensure that each has a clearly defined area of influence.

### OPTIMIZE TRANSPORTATION AND TRAVEL TIME
Assign territories so that vendors can minimize travel time, reducing fatigue and costs.

### INCREASE SALES EFFECTIVENESS
Leverage historical data to identify areas of high performance and areas of untapped potential.

# Analysis of Coverage

Using GIS tools [3] to visualize the geographic distribution of customers and sales helps identify areas of overlap and gaps in coverage. This step is crucial for making informed decisions about spatial subdivision.

### ASSIGNMENT CRITERIA

Criteria for assigning territories should reflect business priorities and market characteristics, such as sales potential, customer density, and ease of access.

### BALANCE AND JUSTICE

Maintaining a balance in the distribution of territories is recommended to ensure that all team members have equivalent opportunities for success. Considerations of equity, workload, and earning potential are critical.

### MONITORING AND ADJUSTMENT

Territory allocation requires periodic revisions to adapt to changes in market and sales performance. Continuous monitoring allows timely changes to be made and the effectiveness of the territory sales strategy to be maintained.

# Proactive Strategies for Assignment.

Introducing proactive strategies can further optimize the allocation of territories:

### USE OF ADVANCED TECHNOLOGY

The adoption of advanced analysis and mapping tools can facilitate partitioning based on sophisticated algorithms that consider multiple variables.

### REGULAR FEEDBACK FROM SELLERS

Encouraging vendors to provide regular feedback on their territories can help quickly identify problems and opportunities.

---

3 *GIS (Geographic Information Systems) tools are software that enable the management, analysis and visualization of geographic data, facilitating map creation and spatial analysis.*

### TRAINING ON LAND MANAGEMENT
Providing specific training to salespeople on territory management principles can increase their efficiency and satisfaction.

## Customization of Strategies

In today's increasingly segmented and diversified marketplace, taking a uniform approach to selling can be ineffective. Customizing sales strategies enables companies to communicate more pertinently with each customer segment, increasing the likelihood of success. Here are some key aspects of this approach:

### DIFFERENTIATED STRATEGIES BY SEGMENT OF CLIENTELE

#### *Identifying Customer Segments*
First, it is crucial to clearly identify and define the various customer segments. This can be based on several criteria, such as demographics, buying behaviors, personal preferences, geographic location, and income level. Analysis of customer data can reveal patterns or behavioral trends that help divide the market into more specific and homogeneous groups. This segmentation allows for better tailoring of marketing and sales strategies, optimizing the approach to each target group in a more effective and targeted way.

#### *Development of Custom Offerings*
Once segments have been identified, the company can develop specific offers for each group. This could include customized products, tailored promotions, and marketing messages calibrated to the segment's preferences and needs. For example, a young, tech-savvy segment might respond better to promotions via app or social media, while a more mature segment might appreciate a direct, personal approach.

#### *Targeted Communication*
Use the communication channels preferred by each segment to send personalized marketing messages. This not only increases the effectiveness of communication, but also the perception of a brand that 'listens' to its customers.

# Vendor Support

### CUSTOM SALES TOOLS
Provide salespeople with tools and materials to help them better understand and serve their customer segments. This includes detailed customer profiles, analysis of their buying behaviors, and guidance on how best to interact with them.

### SEGMENT-SPECIFIC TRAINING
Hold regular training sessions for salespeople focused on sales techniques specific to each customer segment. Training can include simulated sales scenarios, case studies, and role-playing to prepare salespeople for real-world interactions.

### CONTINUOUS FEEDBACK AND ADJUSTMENTS
Implement a system to collect continuous feedback from salespeople on sales strategies. This feedback can be used to further refine strategies and make dynamic adjustments based on sales performance and changes in customer behavior.

# Technology Implementation

### CUSTOM CRMS
Use CRM (customer relationship management) systems[4] advanced to track interactions, preferences, and buying behaviors of customers in each segment. These systems can help automate personalization, making it easier for salespeople to access relevant information in real time.

### ADVANCED ANALYTICS
Invest in analytics solutions that can analyze large amounts of data to identify trends, patterns and opportunities across customer segments. These analytics can guide the

---

4 *Customer Relationship Management (CRM) is a system used by companies to manage and analyze interactions with current and potential customers. It is based on the use of technologies that organize, automate and synchronize sales, marketing, customer service and technical support processes in order to improve business relationships, increase customer satisfaction and optimize revenues.*

personalization strategy and help predict changes in customer behavior.

By taking such a structured, technology-supported approach to personalizing sales strategies, companies can not only improve the effectiveness of their sales initiatives, but also build stronger, longer-lasting relationships with customers. This section of your book will guide readers through the process of transforming their sales operations into a more customer-focused, data-driven business.

# A MORE EFFECTIVE HIERARCHICAL STRUCTURE

In organizing a sales network, the hierarchical structure plays a crucial role in determining the effectiveness and efficiency of the sales force. There are several structures that can be implemented, each with its own advantages and disadvantages, and the choice of the most suitable one depends on various factors, such as the size of the company, the target market, the products or services offered, and the corporate culture. Some of the most popular hierarchical structures are presented below.

## Hierarchical Structures

### TRADITIONAL HIERARCHICAL STRUCTURE

This structure provides for different levels of authority, from sales manager to area managers, regional sales leaders, and field salespeople. It is useful for large organizations with a wide range of products or services because it allows detailed management and direct control over several geographic areas.

### FLAT STRUCTURE

In contrast to the traditional structure, the flat structure reduces the number of hierarchical levels, promoting more direct and rapid communication between management and salespeople. This model is ideal for small and medium-sized companies, as it facilitates flexibility and quick decision-making.

## Functional Structure

In this structure, the sales team is organized according to different functions or roles, such as business development, customer service, or key account management. This organization encourages specialization, but requires effective communication between different departments to ensure that the organization works cohesively and not in watertight compartments.

## Structure in Matrix

It combines elements of functional and product/service structures, where sales teams report to both the sales manager and product or geographic area managers. This structure promotes a high degree of collaboration between departments, but can lead to confusion regarding lines of authority.

## Team-Based Structure

Salespeople are organized into teams focused on specific customers, geographic areas, or market segments. This model fosters a collaborative approach and can be particularly effective in highly competitive or rapidly changing markets.

# **Considerations for Choice of Structure**

The key to a successful sales organization lies in the ability to adapt and react quickly to market changes while maintaining effective communication and strategic alignment within the sales force. There is no universally effective structure; the choice must be based on the company's specific goals, organizational culture and market size. However, many organizations benefit from a structure that integrates elements of different models, thereby responding to market dynamics and customer needs. For example, a company might implement a hierarchical structure for territory management, integrating cross-functional teams to develop specific market segments or products. This hybrid approach allows the strengths of different structures to be combined, providing flexibility and responsiveness.

Territorial division and hierarchy in sales are crucial to effectively allocating territories and managing resources. This requires detailed analysis of market opportunities and customer needs, with a focus on demographic and socioeconomic data. Resource allocation must be proportional and flexible, adapting to market changes. A successful sales structure reflects business objectives and can combine hierarchical territorial management with cross-functional teams to better meet customer needs.

# 3. Selection of the Sales Network

In today's dynamic sales landscape, the selection of sales network members assumes crucial importance.
This process consists of several key steps: from the initial search and pre-selection of candidates, to the final selection and in-depth assessment of their skills and potential. The use of modern technologies, such as Applicant Tracking System (ATS) software[5] and artificial intelligence-based assessment platforms, plays a key role in making this process more efficient.

## Market Statistics and Trends

According to a SalesForce study, 72 percent of companies consider salesperson training and development critical to success in their industry, with LinkedIn research showing a 20 percent increase in sales from well-developed training programs. HubSpot's report shows that the skills most sought after in salespeople today include not only product knowledge and negotiation skills, but also adaptability to new tools and technologies. These data highlight the evolution of sales toward an approach that values digitization and the strategic use of data.

---

5 *Applicant* Tracking *Systems* (ATS) are software that automates recruitment management by facilitating the selection and tracking of applications.

## Evolution of the Salesperson's Role
Statistics suggest that the role of the salesperson is becoming increasingly consultative, with an emphasis on understanding the customer's needs and providing tailored solutions, rather than just the sales transaction.

## Importance of Soft Skills
Another emerging aspect is the importance of soft skills. The ability to establish relationships, empathize with customers, and build trust have become key skills in a modern salesperson's portfolio.

## Adapting to Emerging Technologies
Finally, the ability to adapt to new technologies is critical. Salespeople must be comfortable with tools such as CRM, data analytics platforms, and automated sales systems.

# THE IDEAL CANDIDATE

## Mapping of Specific Competencies
In addition to understanding business needs, it is critical to map the specific skills required for each role in the sales network. This step requires a detailed analysis of the responsibilities of each position, identifying not only the technical skills needed but also the interpersonal skills and personal qualities that foster success in the role.

### Analysis Of The Specific Responsibilities Of The Role
Sales accounts are responsible for managing and developing customer relationships, focusing on sales and long-term goals. It is important to define their responsibilities in detail, which may include generating new business opportunities, negotiating and closing contracts, post-sales follow-up, and handling complaints.

### Development of Custom Profiles
Based on the sales network structure outlined in the first chapter, we develop customized profiles for each role,

requiring close collaboration among the various hierarchical levels to ensure that profiles match actual operational and strategic needs.

## Alignment with Corporate Culture

Compatibility of the ideal profile with the corporate culture is a key factor.

As we map technical skills and personal abilities, it is equally important to assess how these align with the company's values, vision, and mission. A salesperson may have excellent technical skills, but if they do not fit the company culture, they may not reach their full potential.

This aspect underscores the need for a thorough analysis that goes beyond mere technical skills, exploring the behavioral and value aspects that influence integration and collaboration within teams. The selection of candidates should therefore include assessments that examine their affinity for work ethic, communication, teamwork skills, and the long-term vision of the company.

This approach ensures that each team member not only contributes his or her technical expertise but also aligns seamlessly with the corporate environment, thus promoting a cohesive and productive work climate.

## Adaptability to the Market and the Target Customer

Each geographic area and customer segment may require a different approach. In defining the ideal profile, it is important to consider the candidate's ability to adapt to various market contexts and to relate effectively to the target customer.

## Use of Innovative Assessment Tools

To identify candidates who best match the ideal profiles, the use of innovative assessment tools, such as behavioral data analysis and sales simulations, can provide a more accurate picture of their actual skills and potential.

These tools also make it possible to predict the candidate's ability to adapt and grow within the corporate environment.

# WHAT SKILLS?

- Communication and Relationship Skills
- Sector Technical Skills
- Negotiation and Persuasion Skills
- Time Management and Organization
- Adaptability and Continuous Learning
- Resilience and Stress Management
- Customer Orientation and the Solution

These skills need to be assessed not only during the selection phase, but also during the onboarding period[6] and in subsequent phases, to monitor the growth of the resource. The assessment templates to be drafted at the selection stage and then the periodic ones throughout the collaboration period should be based on these basic pillars, through which the bond between the company and its salespeople is strengthened.

# CANDIDATE SEARCH STRATEGIES

We now suggest some strategies for attracting high-quality talent that can strengthen and expand the company's sales capabilities.

## Online Platforms

Job Portals Among the most popular sites such as Indeed, Monster, Infojobs or local job portals where you can post job ads and search for candidates with specific filters.

### SOCIAL MEDIA

Using platforms such as LinkedIn, Facebook, and Twitter allows you to advertise open positions and attract candidates. LinkedIn is particularly useful because of its professional nature and networking features.

---

[6] *Onboarding* is the process of introducing a new human resource to the company, to its culture and way of working. It will be discussed in the dedicated chapter.

## CORPORATE WEB SITES
Creating a "*Work with Us*" section on your company website is essential for posting job ads and receiving direct applications. It is important to ensure that the site communicates a positive image of the company.

# Offline Platforms

### Job Fairs and Networking Events
Attend job fairs, industry conferences, and other networking events to meet potential candidates in person.

### Press and Local Media
Use advertisements in local newspapers or trade magazines to reach candidates who may not be active online.

## SAMPLE ANNOUNCEMENT

### SEARCH
Technology Sales Expert

### DESCRIPTION
*We are looking for an experienced salesperson with strong knowledge in the technology industry. The ideal candidate possesses excellent communication skills, experience selling technology solutions, and a strong drive to achieve goals.*

### KEY REQUIREMENTS
*At least 3 years of experience selling technology products/services. Demonstrated ability to regularly exceed sales goals. Strong customer management and negotiation skills. Familiarity with the use of CRM and sales analysis tools.*

### RESPONSIBILITY
*Manage and develop relationships with existing and new customers. Identify and capitalize on new sales opportunities.*

> *Effectively present and demonstrate technology products.*
> *Provide regular reports on sales performance.*

## USING YOUR NETWORK

Actively engage current employees, business partners, and professional contacts to find candidates by word of mouth. Implement internal referral programs where current employees can recommend professionals from their network.

### Direct Networking

Use your professional networks to identify potential candidates for senior positions. This may include former colleagues, industry contacts, or participants in exclusive networking events.

### External Recommendations

Work with industry associations, universities, and vocational training institutes to receive recommendations of talent that matches the company's requirements.

### Hiring of Professional Headhunters

Hiring specialized headhunting agencies is recommended when we want to identify and approach candidates for senior or highly specialized roles. Headhunters frequently have access to a talent pool that, while not actively seeking new employment, may be interested in meaningful opportunities.

# SELECTION AND EVALUATION

## PRE-SELECTION AND SCREENING

### Initial CV Screening

Use of ATS (or Applicant Tracking System) software to filter CVs based on specific keywords (e.g., "technology sales," "exceeding goals," "CRM"). Manual evaluation of filtered CVs for alignment with company culture and relevant work experience.

### Preliminary Assessment

Sending a pre-interview questionnaire to assess industry knowledge and motivation.

It could be a short, simple online test with Google Forms to assess basic sales and negotiation skills. Or tools such as: *SurveyMonkey, Typeform, Qualtrics, SurveyGizmo, JotForm.*

## *Employment of Advanced Software for Resume Analysis*

The use of advanced software and artificial intelligence systems allows a large volume of resumes to be analyzed efficiently and accurately. These tools can quickly identify candidates who match predefined criteria based on mapping specific skills for the Sales Account role.

### PRE-SELECTION CRITERIA

The software is programmed to recognize specific keywords and phrases that match technical skills, interpersonal and negotiation skills, time management skills, and relevant industry experience. This includes knowledge of specific CRM tools, previous experience in similar roles, and relevant academic qualifications.

### *Evaluation of Past Experiences*

The software assesses not only skills and qualifications, but also the relevance of past work experience. This includes analysis of length of tenure in previous sales roles, the nature of the companies in which candidates have worked (size, industry, etc.), and achievements.

### *Automatic Filtering by Personal Skills and Qualities*

CV analysis systems can also be programmed to identify indicators of interpersonal skills and personal qualities, such as resilience, customer orientation, and adaptability. This can be accomplished through analysis of extracurricular activities, personal projects, or volunteer experiences mentioned in CVs.

### *Integration with Other Assessment Tools*

The screening process does not stop with CV analysis. Systems can be integrated with other assessment tools, such as personality tests or sales simulations, to provide a more comprehensive view of a candidate's potential.

***Saves Time and Improves Effectiveness*** Automating the pre-selection process saves valuable time for the HR team, allowing them to focus on the more qualitative aspects of selection, such as personal interviews and direct interaction with candidates.

## Interview techniques

**INTERVIEW METHODOLOGIES**

We will look at examples of assessment questions and techniques such as behavioral tests, problem-solving exercises, and case analyses. When interviewing and evaluating candidates for the Sales Account role, it is critical to use a combination of methodologies to ensure an accurate assessment of candidates' skills, abilities, and potential.

***Behavioral Interviewing Techniques and Approaches***

This type of interview is based on the principle that past behavior is the best predictor of future behavior. Questions are designed to explore how candidates have dealt with specific situations in the past.

*Examples of Questions*

*"Tell me about a time when you overcame a difficult sales target. And what actions you took."*
*"How did you handle a situation where a customer was dissatisfied? What was the result?"*
*"Describe an experience where you had to work with a team to close a complex sale. What was your specific role on the team?"*
*"What strategies have you adopted to open new markets or acquire new customers in previously uncharted territory?"*
*"What strategies do you use to manage a customer base and how do you ensure their satisfaction and loyalty?"*

## BEHAVIORAL TESTING TECHNIQUES AND APPROACHES
Behavioral tests, such as personality questionnaires or motivation assessment tests, help to better understand candidates' character traits and their suitability for the role.
We recommend tools such as the Myers-Briggs Type Indicator (MBTI)[7] or the Big Five Personality Test[8].

### *Problem-Solving Exercises Techniques and Approaches*
Problem-solving exercises assess candidates' ability to analyze complex situations, think critically and propose effective solutions.

### EXAMPLE PROBLEM SOLVING

*Your company, ABC Technologies, offers innovative software solutions for small and medium-sized enterprises (SMEs) in the retail sector. Recently, ABC Technologies launched a new product that helps retailers improve inventory management efficiency through artificial intelligence. However, many potential customers are still unaware of the concrete benefits this solution can offer or are reluctant to change from their current manual system to an automated one.*

*PROBLEM TO SOLVE*
*As a Sales Account, you are assigned the task of increasing sales of this new product in your territory.*

*YOU FACE TWO MAIN CHALLENGES*
*1) Convince potential customers of the tangible benefits and added value of the new inventory management software.*

---

[7] *The **Myers-Briggs Type Indicator** (MBTI) is a personality test based on Carl Gustav Jung's theory of psychological types. It classifies individuals on the basis of four dimensions, including attitude, basic function, decision-making style and orientation of the external world.*
[8] *The **Big Five Personality Test** assesses personality through five main factors: openness, conscientiousness, extraversion, agreeableness and neuroticism. This model provides an overview of an individual's personality characteristics without categorizing them into specific types.*

2) Overcoming customer objections related to the cost of investment and the learning curve for adopting the new technology.

### ACTIVITIES OF THE CANDIDATE
1) Target Customer Identification
Choose a specific segment of SMEs in the retail sector that could benefit most from the new product.
2) Questions
List 3 questions to gain information and break the ice
3) Development of a Sales Pitch[9]
Create a sales pitch that highlights the benefits of the product, such as reducing inventory waste, optimizing inventory, and improving operational efficiency.
4) Include concrete examples or case studies.

### MANAGEMENT OF OBJECTIONS
Prepare responses to possible objections, such as concerns about the cost of implementation or doubts about the ease of use of the software.
1) Proposed Gradual Implementation Plan.
2) Develop a proposal for a phased implementation of the software that minimizes disruption to the client's current operations and provides initial training to ease the transition.

### MEASURING SUCCESS
Define key performance indicators (KPIs) to evaluate the effectiveness of the sales pitch and the success of product implementation with new customers.

---

[9] In sales, a **pitch** is a short persuasive presentation used to communicate the benefits and features of a product or service to a potential customer, with the goal of generating interest and convincing him or her to buy.

# Selling Skill Evaluation

## SALES SIMULATION (ROLE-PLAYING)

The candidate should simulate a sales situation in which he/she presents his/her pitch to a "customer" (played by a member of the evaluation team). The simulation should include presenting the product, handling the client's objections, and discussing the implementation plan. This activity will assess the candidate's direct selling skills, his ability to effectively communicate the benefits of the product, and to negotiate solutions that meet the customer's needs. Before starting, it is advisable to create a relaxed environment because some emotional people may be more uncomfortable than they would be in everyday reality.

## FEEDBACK AND DECISION

The post-interview feedback and decision-making process is critical in the recruitment cycle, allowing candidates to be evaluated in an objective and informed manner to identify the best fit for the open position.

## COLLECTION AND DOCUMENTATION OF FEEDBACK

After each interview or assessment, it is important that all interview panel members or those who conducted the assessment complete structured feedback. This may include:

### *Quantitative Evaluations*

Assign standardized scores for each competency assessed during the interview or exercise, based on a predefined scale (e.g., 1 to 5).

### *Qualitative Observations*

Note specific impressions, examples of candidate responses that demonstrate particular skills or areas for improvement, and any notes regarding the candidate's cultural fit with the company.

### *Comparison with the Ideal Profile*

Compare the feedback collected for each candidate with the ideal profile defined in the skills mapping phase in terms of technical knowledge, experience, soft skills, and alignment with company values.

## COLLECTIVE DISCUSSION

Hold a final meeting of the selection process with all members of the interview committee to discuss the candidates. This time of sharing allows for:

### *Integrate different perspectives and reduce bias[10] individuals*

Evaluate candidates' performance overall, discussing discrepancies in feedback and reaching consensus. Identify any need for additional information or clarification (e.g., a second interview on specific aspects).

### *Use of Decision Matrices*

To facilitate decision making, it may be useful to use decision matrices[11] that include the main evaluation criteria and scores assigned to each candidate. These tools help to clearly visualize where candidates rank against the requirements of the role and with each other.

### *Cultural Fit and Growth Potential*

In addition to technical skills and experience, carefully assess the candidate's cultural fit or fit with the company and potential for growth. These aspects are critical to ensure that the candidate can integrate and contribute positively over the long term.

## FINAL DECISION AND COMMUNICATION

After reaching a consensus, proceed with the final decision. It is important-often companies fall into this communication gaffe-to inform all candidates of the decision in a timely manner, offering constructive feedback to those not selected, in order to maintain a good corporate image and help them in their career growth. Better an automated email to notify the candidate that the position is closed than to ignore it altogether.

---

10 **Bias** *is a bias or distortion in perception or judgment that influences decisions and actions in ways that are not rational or impartial.*

11 *For example a famous matrix is Adenauer Cross, named after German politician Konrad Adenauer who used it to make important decisions. In this area, it is called* **the Personnel Priority Matrix**. *This matrix divides candidates according to two main dimensions: competence and cultural fit.*

In today's environment of constant change and technological innovation, the careful selection of the sales network becomes increasingly crucial. Using advanced tools and targeted strategies to recruit competent salespeople aligned with the corporate culture ensures substantial competitive advantages and continuous improvement in business performance.

# 4. Onboarding

Onboarding is the gradual and systematic process of integrating a new resource into a company. The goal is to facilitate the integration of the newly hired employee by providing him or her with all the information and tools necessary to be operational and efficient as soon as possible. In fact, the quicker and more effective the new resource's onboarding is, the less time it will take to achieve sales network goals.

## PRE-ONBOARDING

Even before the first day, send the new hire a welcome packet that may include a new-hire guide, company-related documentation, and a detailed plan for the first few weeks. This step helps reduce first-day anxiety and demonstrates the company's organization and welcome.

## **First Day of Work**

Make sure the first day is well structured. This can include a tour of the office, presentation to team members and key stakeholders, and an orientation session about the company, its history, culture, and values.

Provide everything you need to get started: workstation, access to computer systems, and work materials.

## Detailed Orientation Program

Develop an orientation program covering the first few weeks or months. This should include training sessions on the company's products or services, sales processes, CRM tools, and company policies. Incorporate training sessions on soft skills, such as effective communication, time management, and conflict resolution.

## Assignment of a Mentor or Buddy

Pair the new hire with an experienced mentor or "buddy" within the sales team. This person can provide informal support, answer questions and help the new member navigate the company culture. The mentor can also assist the new hire with hands-on activities, such as sales simulations or reviewing case studies.

# The Mansionary

In industry, every step in the production process is crucial to ensuring the quality of the finished product. Similarly, in the sales process, every step, from lead generation to deal closing, must be executed with precision and attention to detail.

The "Job description" is a detailed compilation of the tasks that each salesperson must perform in the sales process.

### Example Sales Process

***Preparation***
*Market analysis, product/service study, target customer identification.*

***Prospecting***
*Prospect research and lead qualification.*

***Approach***
*First contact with the potential client, whether direct (phone call, in-person meeting) or indirect (email, social media).*

***Needs Assessment***

> *Understanding of customer needs through targeted questions and active listening.*
>
> ***BID PRESENTATION***
> *Demonstration of product/service value in response to identified needs.*
>
> ***OBJECTION MANAGEMENT***
> *Identifying and overcoming resistance to purchase.*
>
> ***CLOSING***
> *Conclusion of the deal by negotiating the terms and signing the contract.*
>
> ***FOLLOW-UP***
> *Maintaining after-sales contact to ensure customer satisfaction and promote future sales.*

### REGULAR FEEDBACK AND CHECK-IN

Schedule regular feedback meetings between the new hire and his or her manager or human resources manager. These check-ins are essential to discuss progress, address any challenges, and tailor the onboarding program to the new member's specific needs. Regular feedback helps keep the lines of communication open and strengthen a sense of team ownership.

### EVALUATION OF THE ONBOARDING EXPERIENCE

At the end of the orientation program, gather feedback from the new hire on the onboarding experience. This can help identify areas for improvement and refine the process for future team members.

## ACTIVE INVOLVEMENT

### TEAM BUILDING INITIATIVES

Organize team-building activities that encourage collaboration and communication between new hires and members

Of the existing team. This can include interactive workshops, team retreats, or simple social gatherings such as shared lunches or coffees. Team building activities help to break the ice, build professional and personal relationships, and facilitate team integration.

## IMMERSION IN CORPORATE CULTURE

Introduce new hires to the company culture through dedicated sessions exploring the company's values, mission, and vision. Share company success stories and examples of how values have been put into practice in daily work.

Involve corporate leaders in these sessions to emphasize the importance of corporate culture and to show management's commitment to welcoming new members.

## MENTORSHIP AND ONGOING SUPPORT

Extend the mentorship program beyond the first few weeks, allowing new hires to have a constant point of reference for questions or to discuss professional challenges.

The mentor or buddy can help the new member navigate the corporate culture, offering advice on how to interact effectively within the team and the larger organization.

## PARTICIPATION IN CORPORATE INITIATIVES

Encourage new hires to actively participate in company initiatives, such as working groups on specific issues, committees for social events, or company-sponsored volunteer programs. Participation in these initiatives can accelerate integration into the corporate culture, allowing new members to contribute their own ideas and feel an integral part of the organization.

## FEEDBACK AND CONTINUOUS EVALUATION

Implement an ongoing feedback process that allows new hires to express their opinions and perceptions about their experience integrating into the team and company. Use this feedback to improve integration strategies and to ensure that new members feel heard and valued.

## RECOGNITION AND CELEBRATION OF SUCCESSES
Recognize and celebrate the successes of new hires, both individually and as part of the team. This may include achievement of sales goals, contribution to successful projects, or demonstrated commitment to professional learning and growth. Public recognition of successes helps to strengthen new members' sense of belonging and motivation.

# The Mentor

## MENTOR SELECTION

### Selection Criteria
Identify and select internal mentors based on experience, leadership skills, communication skills and, most importantly, willingness to share knowledge and invest in the success of others.

### Mentor Training
Provide mentors with specific training that prepares them for their role, including insights into the onboarding process, effective mentoring techniques, and how to provide constructive feedback.

## MENTOR-MENTEE PAIRING

### Compatibility
Match new hires with mentors based on professional compatibility and, if possible, personal interests to facilitate a productive and positive relationship.

### Learning Objectives.
Clearly define learning and development goals, ensuring that they are aligned with the new hire's career goals and business needs.

## STRUCTURING THE MENTORING PROGRAM

### Regular Meeting Plan
Establish a regular cadence for meetings between mentor and mentee, either formally (e.g., weekly or monthly meetings) or informally (e.g., lunches).

### Meeting Agenda

Meetings should have a flexible agenda that includes reviewing progress, discussing specific challenges, sharing useful resources, and planning future goals.

## MONITORING AND SUPPORT

### Continuous Feedback
Encourage a culture of continuous feedback within the mentoring relationship, allowing the mentee to freely express concerns and the mentor to offer timely advice.

### Periodic Evaluation
Conduct periodic evaluations of the mentoring relationship to ensure that it is productive and responsive to the mentee's needs, making changes if necessary.

## INTEGRATION WITH THE ONBOARDING PROGRAM

### Linking with Other Initiatives
Ensure that the mentoring program is well integrated with other phases of the onboarding process, such as technical training and cultural immersion, to provide a cohesive experience.

## RECOGNITION OF MENTOR COMMITMENT

### Appreciation and Recognition
Recognize and celebrate the commitment and contribution of mentors with formal appreciation, awards, or recognition, valuing their key role in the success of the onboarding program.

> Chapter 4 outlines a meticulous approach to onboarding, emphasizing the importance of structured induction for new hires. The strategy combines technical orientation, soft skills, and mentorship to accelerate integration and maximize productivity.
> This is an exemplary model that ensures immediate impact and continued growth.

# 5. Training Pathways

An important role in the life and development of a sales network is played by continuing education. We have already seen how important it is today to have a sales team that is always up-to-date and prepared for the challenges of the market. Below we will provide concrete examples of training courses that can be provided as early as the onboarding phase, but which could be extremely useful to more experienced employees as well.

## TRAINING PROGRAM HYPOTHESIS

### Course on the Company's Products/Services

**COURSE OBJECTIVE.**
Provide a complete and thorough understanding of the products or services offered by the company. This includes details on technical features, distinctive advantages, market positioning, and practical applications or specific use cases.

**STRUCTURE OF THE MODULE**

*Introduction to Products/Services*
Detailed presentation of products/services, including development history, evolution over time, and company vision.

Explanation of key technical features and how they differ from competing products/services.

## Customer Benefits and Advantages

In-depth analysis of the benefits that products/services bring to customers, with practical examples of success and testimonials. Interactive sessions on how to effectively communicate these benefits to potential customers.

## Practical Applications and Use Cases

Study of real use cases demonstrating how products/services solved specific customer problems. Group exercises to develop customized value propositions for different customer scenarios.

## Comparison with Competition

Comparative analysis with major competitors, highlighting strengths and areas for improvement. Role-play on how to handle objections from customers considering alternative products/services today.

## Supporting Technologies and Innovations

Training on the underlying technologies that support the products/services, including any software, platforms, or hardware. Workshops on future innovations and how they might affect the company's offerings.

# TRAINING METHODOLOGIES

## Classroom and Online Training

Combine classroom sessions with online training materials to provide flexible, self-directed learning.

## Practical Demonstrations

Use live or virtual demonstrations to show the use of products/services in realistic settings.

## Q&A Sessions

Regularly schedule question-and-answer sessions to clarify doubts and explore complex issues.

# EVALUATION AND FEEDBACK

## Knowledge Test

Implement periodic tests to assess understanding of products/services and identify areas that require further training.

***Continuous Feedback***
Gather feedback from participants to continuously improve technical training modules.

# Sales and Negotiation Techniques

## GOALS

Develop participants' persuasive communication skills, enabling them to present products/services convincingly. Teach effective negotiation strategies that enable salespeople to reach mutually beneficial agreements. Provide techniques for overcoming customer objections, turning doubts into sales opportunities.

## COMPONENTS OF THE MODULE

### *Fundamentals of Consultative Selling*

Introduction to the concept of consultative selling, which emphasizes creating value for the customer and establishing long-term relationships. How to actively listen.

### *Effective Communication Techniques*

Sessions on how to use verbal and nonverbal communication to establish rapport and build trust with customers. Role-play to practice using open-ended questions, active listening and presenting product/service benefits clearly and persuasively.

### *Negotiation Strategies*

Interactive workshops on negotiation techniques, including preparation for negotiation, setting negotiation goals, and managing negotiations. Case studies illustrating successful and less successful negotiations, with discussion of key points for success.

### *Handling Objections and Closing the Sale*
Specific training on how to anticipate, recognize and respond effectively to customer objections. Techniques of

closing of the sale that help guide the customer to the final decision while maintaining a solution-oriented approach.

## LEARNING METHODS

### Sales Simulations
Create simulated sales scenarios that reflect real situations, allowing participants to practice the techniques learned in a controlled environment.

### Constructive Feedback
Provide immediate and constructive feedback after each role-play or exercise, highlighting strengths and areas for improvement.

### Peer Learning
Encourage the sharing of experiences and strategies among participants, promoting a collaborative learning environment.

## EVALUATION AND CONTINUOUS IMPROVEMENT

### Assessment of Competencies
Use pre- and post-training evaluations to measure participants' progress in sales and negotiation techniques.

### Feedback from Participants
Gather feedback on the content, structure and effectiveness of the training module to identify areas for improvement and adapt the program to future needs.

# Effective Communication and Active Listening

## WORKSHOP OBJECTIVES.
Improve salespeople's ability to communicate clearly and persuasively, both in sales and interpersonal settings within the company. Develop active listening. Provide participants with practical techniques to immediately apply these skills in their daily work.

## COMPONENTS OF THE WORKSHOP

### Fundamentals of Effective Communication

Introduction to the basic principles of effective communication, including verbal and nonverbal language, message structuring, and the importance of feedback. Discussion of the impact of communication barriers and how to overcome them.

### *Active Listening Practices*

Practice focused on active listening, teaching participants how to give full attention to the speaker, understand the message, respond appropriately, and remember key information. Role-plays to practice active listening in sales scenarios, with constructive feedback from facilitators and peers.

### *Persuasive Communication*

Techniques on how to construct persuasive arguments, tailor the message to the audience, and use stories and examples to connect emotionally with the listener. Analysis of case studies demonstrating effective persuasive communications in the sales context.

### *Managing Objections through Communication*

Strategies for anticipating and responding to customer objections constructively, turning potential resistance into opportunities to deepen the discussion.

Simulations of real situations where participants can practice handling common objections, with the goal of strengthening the customer relationship.

### *Feedback and Internal Communication*

Importance of constructive feedback within the sales team and strategies for giving and receiving feedback effectively. Interactive workshops on how to improve internal communication, including information sharing, conflict resolution, and mutual support among colleagues.

## METHODOLOGY AND TOOLS

### *Interactive Approach*

Use a mix of lectures, group discussions, hands-on exercises and role-play to ensure active and engaging learning.

### *Supporting Materials*

Provide participants with guides, checklists and reference materials to support the practice of effective communication and active listening beyond the workshop.

### *Evaluation Continued*
Implement moments of evaluation and self-assessment to enable participants to reflect on their progress and identify areas for improvement.

## Customer Relations Management

### MODULE OBJECTIVES.
Equip Sales Accounts with effective strategies for building and maintaining long-term customer relationships. Develop skills in managing customer expectations and proactive problem solving. Teach techniques for strengthening customer trust and loyalty, creating a solid foundation for future sales opportunities and referrals.

### COMPONENTS OF THE MODULE

#### *Customer Relationship Management (CRM)*
Overview of key CRM principles, including listening to customer needs, personalizing interactions, and the importance of a service-oriented approach. Use of CRM systems to monitor customer interactions, manage customer data, and analyze buying patterns to deliver targeted solutions.

#### *Effective and Personalized Communication*
Techniques for communicating effectively with different types of customers, including adaptability of communication style and use of positive language. Training on how to personalize communication based on customer preferences and purchase history to show understanding and attention to detail.

#### *Building Trust and Managing Loyalty*
Strategies for building trust through transparency, reliability, and consistency in interactions. Discussion of how trust influences customer loyalty and how to maintain long-term relationships through excellent customer service and loyalty initiatives.

### *Proactive Troubleshooting*
Methods for anticipating and identifying potential problems in customer relationships and techniques for dealing with them proactively and constructively. Role-plays on real problem-solving scenarios, with the goal of preserving customer trust and turning challenges into opportunities for improvement.

### *Customer Feedback and Continuous Improvement*
Importance of customer feedback as a tool for continuous improvement of sales and relationship strategies. Techniques for collecting, analyzing, and acting on customer feedback, including implementing changes based on customer needs and preferences.

## LEARNING METHODS
### *Interactive Workshops and Group Discussions*
Create a collaborative learning environment where participants can share experiences and strategies.

### *Practical Exercises*
Use exercises and simulations to put the techniques learned into practice, with a special focus on relationship management and problem solving.

## EVALUATION AND FEEDBACK
### *Practical Assessment*
Implement assessments based on practical exercises and role-play to measure the effective application of acquired skills.

### *Continuous Feedback*
Gather feedback from participants to refine and improve the training module.

# Time Management and Work Organization

## MODULE OBJECTIVES.
Teach participants to identify and focus on high-value-added activities, minimizing distractions and effectively managing interruptions. Provide tools and techniques for a

optimal work planning and organization, enabling salespeople to better manage their schedules and increase productivity.
Develop skills to set and achieve realistic goals, improving time management and job satisfaction.

## COMPONENTS OF THE MODULE

### *Fundamental Principles of Time Management*
Introduction to key concepts of time management, such as the importance of setting priorities, the difference between urgent and important tasks, and techniques for avoiding procrastination.
Discussion of common time management pitfalls and how to avoid them.

### *Tools and Techniques of Organization*
Presentation of planning tools, both digital (time management apps, project management software) and analog (diaries, planners), highlighting the pros and cons of each.
Hands-on workshops on how to use these tools to organize your workday, set goals, and monitor progress.

### *Planning and Prioritization*
Exercises on how to identify daily and weekly priorities, including the technique of *Time Blocking*[12] for allocating blocks of time to specific tasks. Strategies for addressing and scaling complex tasks into manageable actions.

### *Effective Delegation and Interruption Management*
Training on how to delegate nonessential tasks to focus on those that require the salesperson's specific expertise. Techniques for handling common interruptions and distractions while maintaining focus on the tasks at hand.

### *Balance between Professional and Personal Life*
Discusses the importance of maintaining a healthy work-life balance, and how good time management can contribute to this balance. Suggestions for

---

12 *Time* **blocking** *is a time management technique of dividing the workday into blocks of time assigned to specific activities or tasks. This method helps to better organize time, increase productivity and reduce distractions. You plan in advance when and how much time you will devote to each task, thus promoting a more disciplined and intentional approach to work.*

disconnect from work and regain energy, overall improving productivity and well-being.

## LEARNING METHODS

### Active Learning
Incorporate hands-on activities, group exercises and real-life case discussions to enable participants to directly apply the techniques learned.

### Coaching Sessions
Offer individual or small group coaching sessions to address personal challenges in time management and work organization.

## EVALUATION AND FEEDBACK

### Self-evaluation
Encourage participants to reflect on their time management practices before and after the course, evaluating improvements and identifying future goals.

### Continuous Feedback
Collect feedback from participants at the end of the course to evaluate its effectiveness and make any improvements.

# Problem Solving and Stress Management

## MODULE OBJECTIVES.
Develop the ability to quickly identify root causes of problems and apply creative and effective solutions. Teach stress management techniques to help salespeople stay focused and productive even in high-pressure situations.

Improve personal resilience, enabling salespeople to deal with challenges and failures as opportunities for growth.

## COMPONENTS OF THE MODULE

### Problem Solving Techniques
Introduction to problem solving models and strategies, such as "*Lateral Thinking*" and Edward de Bono's "*Six Hats Method for Thinking*"[13], to stimulate the creative approach to

---

[13] **Edward de Bono** *was a Maltese psychologist and author known for his work on lateral thinking and techniques for improving decision making and creativity to encourage creative problem solving.*

problem solving. Hands-on workshops that simulate complex sales scenarios, where participants must identify innovative solutions to the challenges presented.

### *Stress Management*
Training on the causes of stress in the sales context and how to recognize signs of stress in oneself and colleagues.
Stress reduction techniques, including meditation exercises, breathing techniques, and time management, to help salespeople maintain emotional balance and mental clarity.

### *Resilience and Adaptability*
Sessions focused on developing resilience, teaching salespeople how to maintain a positive attitude in the face of difficulties and how to adapt quickly to change.
Discussion of strategies for turning failures and criticism into opportunities for learning and growth.

### *Communication in Stressful Situations*
Exercises on how to maintain effective communication with clients and colleagues even under pressure, including handling difficult conversations and negotiating in tense situations.
Role-play to practice empathetic and assertive communication, focusing on maintaining positive relationships even in challenging circumstances.

## LEARNING METHODOLOGIES

### *Learning by Doing*
Learning by doing. Use a hands-on approach, with exercises, simulations and role-plays that allow participants to immediately put the skills they have learned into practice.

### *Group Sessions and Individual Reflection*
Encourage group discussion to share experiences and strategies, as well as individual reflection time to personalize stress management techniques.

## EVALUATION AND FEEDBACK

### *Self-Assessment and Peer Feedback*
Encourage regular self-assessments and peer feedback to monitor progress in problem solving and stress management.

### *Follow-up and Ongoing Support*
Offer follow-up sessions or one-on-one coaching to support continued application of learned strategies in daily work life.

# LEARNING TECHNIQUES

## **Role Playing and Sales Simulations**

### OBJECTIVES OF THE ACTIVITY
Provide salespeople with opportunities to practice sales and negotiation techniques in realistic scenarios. Help salespeople develop and hone their soft skills, such as active listening, effective communication, and objection handling.
Increase salespeople's confidence in their ability to interact with customers, preparing them to handle a variety of sales situations.

### STRUCTURE OF THE ACTIVITY
Preparation and Briefing Identify specific learning objectives for each role playing or simulation session, based on the skills you want to develop or improve. Create sales scenarios based on real-world situations, including different types of customers, common objections, and sales challenges.

### ASSIGNMENT OF ROLES
Assign participants specific roles, alternating between the role of the salesperson and that of the customer or other stakeholders involved in the sales process. Provide "customers" with detailed briefings on their background, needs and potential objections to make the simulation as realistic as possible.

### CONDUCTING SIMULATIONS
Conduct the simulations in an environment that encourages mutual respect and support, allowing vendors to experiment and take initiative. Record the sessions to allow for detailed review and constructive feedback later.

## DEBRIEFING AND FEEDBACK

After each role playing session, organize a debriefing[14] group debriefing to discuss what went well, areas for improvement, and lessons learned. Provide specific and constructive feedback to each participant, highlighting strengths and suggesting ways to address areas of weakness.

## REPETITION AND PRACTICE

Encourage repetition of simulations with varied scenarios and roles to expose salespeople to a wider range of situations. Use follow-up sessions to practice feedback received and demonstrate improvement over time.

## BENEFITS OF THE ACTIVITY

Improved sales skills through practice and repetition in a low-risk environment. Increased understanding of and empathy for customer perspectives and challenges. Development of the ability to think quickly and adapt to unexpected situations during the sales process.

# **One-To-One Coaching Sessions**

## OBJECTIVES OF THE SESSIONS

Provide personalized support to salespeople to help them achieve their professional goals and improve sales performance. Identify and develop strategies to overcome specific individual challenges, both at the technical and soft skill level. Enhance salespeople's motivation and engagement through tailored professional development.

## STRUCTURING OF THE SESSIONS

### *Goal Setting*

At the beginning of the coaching journey, set clear and measurable goals with the salesperson for the sessions, based on their professional aspirations and identified development needs. Goals can range from acquiring new

---

14 ***Debriefing*** *is a process of reflection and discussion following an activity or event, aimed at examining outcomes, discussing successes and mistakes, and identifying lessons for improving future performance.*

sales skills, to improving time management, to developing greater resilience.

### *Sessions Planning*
Schedule regular sessions, such as monthly or quarterly, to ensure ongoing support and monitor progress toward established goals. Ensure that each session is prepared in advance, with a specific agenda based on progress made and topics to be explored.

### *Conducting Sessions*
Use active listening techniques to deeply understand the salesperson's experiences, perceptions, and challenges. Apply powerful questions to stimulate reflection, self-awareness, and discovery of personal solutions to challenges faced. Provide constructive feedback, resources and practical tools to support seller development.

### *Developing and Implementing Action Plans*
Work with the salesperson to develop detailed action plans that address development goals, with specific actions, deadlines and indicators of success. Encourage implementation of what is learned in daily sales activities to promote continuous improvement.

### *Monitoring Progress and Adaptation*
Regularly assess progress toward established goals and discuss challenges encountered in implementing action plans. Adjust development goals and strategies based on feedback and changes in vendor needs or priorities.

### *Benefits of One-to-One Coaching Sessions.*
Individual coaching sessions offer many benefits, including targeted development of individual skills. This type of individualized training has a significant impact on sales performance by addressing and enhancing specific areas of improvement for each salesperson. In addition, salespeople feel more motivated and engaged in their professional development.

# Peer-To-Peer Study and Learning Groups

## OBJECTIVES OF THE ACTIVITY

Foster through a two-way mode the sharing of knowledge, sales strategies and best practices among peer-to-peer members of the sales network. Develop skills through exposure to different perspectives and
solutions to common problems. Strengthen the sense of belonging and build a corporate culture based on collaboration and continuous learning.

## STRUCTURING OF THE ACTIVITY

### *Formation of Groups*

Create study groups or learning circles based on common interests, specific challenges or development goals.
Make sure the groups are small enough to allow active participation by all members, but diverse enough to ensure a variety of perspectives.

### *Selection of Themes*

Identify relevant topics for training and development, which may range from advanced sales techniques, time management, to soft skills such as effective communication or resilience. Encourage group members to propose topics based on their own experiences and learning needs.

### *Organization of Sessions*

Schedule regular meetings, both virtual and in-person, where members can discuss selected topics, share experiences, and collaborate on problem solving. Alternate facilitator roles among group members to promote engagement and individual accountability.

### *Collaborative Learning Methods*

Use a variety of learning methods, including case studies, role-playing, simulation games, and commentary on texts from relevant literature. Promote the use of online learning platforms to share resources, teaching materials, and to facilitate discussion between sessions.

### *Feedback and Reflection*

Encourage constructive peer feedback at the end of each session to reinforce strengths and identify areas for improvement. Set aside time for individual and group reflection on what was learned and how to apply it in the work context.

## BENEFITS PEER-TO-PEER LEARNING AND GROUPS OF STUDIO

### *Increased Retention of Learning*[15]

Collaborative learning and peer teaching tend to improve retention of information and practical application of acquired skills.

### *Creative Solutions to Problems*

Diversity of perspectives within groups can stimulate creative and innovative solutions to sales problems.

### *Support and Motivation*

Group learning provides a level of emotional and motivational support, encouraging salespeople to overcome challenges together.

---

In Chapter 5, it is explained how the use of structured and defined training paths, both in onboarding and for experienced employees, significantly impacts sales network development. These pathways include product/service understanding, advanced sales techniques, and customer relationship management. Continuing education improves technical and interpersonal skills, strengthening team cohesion and resilience, contributing to the company's growth and sustainable success.

---

15  *Learning retention refers to an individual's ability to remember and use learned information and skills over time. In other words, it indicates how well and how long a person can retain and recall what he or she has learned.*

# 6. Goal Setting

Setting clear and measurable goals, along with creating fair and ethical incentive plans, are crucial components for motivating the sales network and stimulating performance. There is no improvement unless an end point is identified: the goal. That in the case of a sales team, not only serves as a guiding beacon for the daily activities of the sales team, but also offer a criterion for measuring the success of the sales strategies implemented.

## CONTEXT ANALYSIS

Begin with a thorough analysis of the company's business environment, market trends and overall strategic goals. This will help ensure that sales goals are aligned with the company's direction. It is the key starting point for setting effective sales goals that are aligned with the company's overall strategy. This process helps ensure that sales activities not only contribute to the achievement of immediate revenue goals [16], but also support the long-term vision and sustainable growth of the organization.

---

16  *The term **Revenue** is used in economics in reference to revenue, which is the total revenue generated by a company through its main operating activity, before subtracting any costs or expenses.*

## LET'S HAVE CLARITY

It is time to dispel a myth: the sales manager is not just the "sales captain." If we are to be honest and accurate, a sales manager's job definition should include not only driving sales, but also managing the costs and financial resources allocated to his or her department. Yet, how many organizations actually give this figure responsibility for spending?

The reality is that there are few, very few companies that entrust the sales manager with real spending power. This means that although he or she is universally recognized for the turnover he or she brings in, he or she is just as rarely valued for the Gross Operating Margin (GOM) he or she manages to generate. M.O.L., for the uninitiated, measures operating profit before finance charges and taxes, offering a much more comprehensive view than just sales volume.
Ignoring this indicator is like evaluating a cook only by the quantity of dishes served, without considering the quality of ingredients and cost of preparation.

Therefore, it is crucial to recognize that the true value of a sales manager is not measured only in terms of sales, but rather in his or her ability to increase corporate profitability. A successful sales manager is not the one who sells the most, but the one who knows how to optimize costs, manage resources and, as a result, increase the company's M.O.L.

In conclusion, if we really want to value the role of the sales manager, we need to start evaluating not only how much he or she sells, but how much he or she contributes to making the company more profitable. Only then can we give this figure the recognition it deserves and, more importantly, guide our companies toward a future of greater efficiency and profitability.

# Steps for Business Context Analysis

### REVIEW OF CORPORATE MISSION AND VISION.
Begin by reviewing the company's mission and vision to ensure that any proposed sales objectives are in line with these guiding principles. This ensures consistency and integrity between sales activities and core company values.

### ASSESSMENT OF OVERALL STRATEGIC GOALS
Analyze the company's long-term strategic goals, which might include expansion into new markets, launching new products or services, or improving market share in key areas. Sales objectives should directly support these strategic goals.

### REVIEW OF PAST PERFORMANCE
Conduct an analysis of past sales performance, identifying trends, areas of strength and weakness, and any gaps between goals and actual results. This can provide insights[17] valuable for future goal setting.

### ANALYSIS OF MARKET TRENDS
Study current and expected market trends, including consumer behaviors, technological innovations, and competitive movements. This helps identify potential opportunities and threats that may influence sales objectives.

### ASSESSMENT OF AVAILABLE RESOURCES
Consider available resources, including the skills of the sales team, marketing budget, and technology infrastructure. Sales goals should be realistic relative to the resources that can be allocated.

---

17 An *"insight"* *is a profound and often sudden understanding or revelation that provides a new perspective or way of looking at a situation, problem or data. It can be translated as insight, cues or suggestions.*

### Stakeholder Involvement
Include various business stakeholders, such as the product, marketing, finance, and operations teams, in the analysis process to ensure that sales goals are aligned with the cross-functional functions of the company.

## Implementation Of The Analysis
### Documentation and Communication
Clearly document the results of the analysis and communicate them to sales teams and other relevant stakeholders. This ensures that everyone is aligned and understands how sales goals fit into the larger business context.

### Continuous Feedback
Keep communication channels open for continuous feedback during the implementation of sales goals. This allows adjustments to be made based on changes in the business or market environment.

## "SMART" GOALS
The acronym SMART indicates that objectives should be Specific, Measurable, Achievable, Relevant, and Timed. This approach ensures that each salesperson knows exactly what he or she will be evaluated on. SMART Goal Development for salespeople is a process that ensures clarity, focus, and measurability of the goals to be achieved.

## S for Specific
### Clarity of Objectives
Goals should be clearly and comprehensibly defined. Instead of having a generic goal such as "increase sales," specify "increase sales by 15 percent in the SMB (small business) customer segment by Q4."

### Important Details
Include key details such as target customers, specific product or service, and geographic region of focus.

## M for Measurable

### QUANTIFYING THE OBJECTIVE
Ensure that each goal has a quantifiable parameter, such as a number or percentage, to enable performance evaluation.

### MEASUREMENT TOOLS
Define the tools and metrics that will be used to track progress, such as CRM software to track sales or customer feedback to assess satisfaction.

## A for Achievable

### REALISM
Goals should be ambitious but realistic, taking into account available resources, vendor skills, and market conditions.

### SUPPORT AND RESOURCES
Identifying the resources, support, and training needed to help salespeople achieve their goals is critical. It is important to provide salespeople with the right tools and access to training programs that will enhance their skills and knowledge.

## R for Relevant.

### ALIGNMENT WITH CORPORATE GOALS
Sales goals must be consistent with the company's overall strategic goals, thus contributing to its vision and mission.

### MOTIVATION
Ensure that goals are meaningful to the salesperson, increasing personal motivation and commitment toward their achievement.

## T for Time-bound (Temporally Defined)

### CLEAR DEADLINES
Each goal should have a specific deadline, which provides a sense of urgency and helps plan sales activity.

## PERIODIC REVIEWS
Establish periodic reviews to assess progress toward the goal and make any adjustments.

# Implementing SMART Goals.

## EFFECTIVE COMMUNICATION
Present SMART goals to vendors clearly and make sure there is mutual understanding.

## FEEDBACK AND ADAPTATION
Maintain a flexible approach, adapting goals based on feedback received and changes in the business or market environment.

# Customizing Goals

In certain contexts, it is appropriate to consider tailoring goals to each salesperson's skills, experience level and sales territory. This increases the perception of equity and individual motivation. Goal Personalization is an extremely relevant strategy for optimizing sales network performance. Recognizing that each salesperson has a unique set of skills, experiences, and specific challenges related to their territory, personalization aims to create goals that are not only attainable but also challenging for the individual.

## STEPS FOR GOAL CUSTOMIZATION

### *Individual Analysis*
Begin with a detailed analysis of each salesperson's skills, past performance and experience level. Also assess conditions specific to the sales territory, such as market potential and competition.

### *Dialogue with Vendors*
Involving salespeople in defining their goals helps to identify their professional aspirations, perceptions of the challenges in the area, and the areas in which they wish to develop. In this way, each salesperson feels that he or she is an active part of the team and the company's strategy, thereby increasing their sense of belonging and motivation.

### Tailored Goal Setting
On the basis of analysis and dialogue but always keeping in mind the group's objective to decline to each subject, tailored sales goals that take into account individual peculiarities: sales volumes, acquisition of new customers or growth rates, to each seller and territory.

### Flexibility and Adaptability
Maintain flexibility in goals, allowing adjustments based on changing market conditions, ongoing feedback and vendor progress.

### Support and Resources
Ensure that salespeople have access to the resources, training, and support they need to achieve their customized goals such as product-specific information materials, advanced training on sales techniques, or assistance in improving time management.

### Monitoring and Evaluation
Establish a monitoring and evaluation system that reflects the personalized nature of the goals Periodic meetings and if necessary, recalibrate the goals.

## BENEFITS OF PERSONALIZATION GOALS

### Increased Motivation
Customized goals are perceived as more relevant and achievable by salespeople, increasing their motivation and commitment.

### Optimized Performance
Customization enables the best use of each salesperson's skills, optimizing the overall performance of the sales network.

### Job Satisfaction
Consideration of individual aspirations and provision of development opportunities contribute to vendor satisfaction and loyalty.

### Perceived Equity

Customizing goals demonstrates a corporate commitment to recognizing and supporting individual needs, promoting a sense of equity within the team. The concept of equity is highly felt among salespeople, which if mishandled can create a sense of injustice and rift with management that is difficult to mend.

# PERFORMANCE MONITORING

Provide an objective and continuous evaluation of the performance of each member of the sales network, based on clear and predefined metrics. Identify areas of strength and those in need of development, allowing customization of training and growth plans. Motivate salespeople through recognition of their achievements and support in their professional improvement journey.

## Components of the Process

### SETTING CLEAR METRICS AND GOALS

Establishing performance goals together with salespeople[18] is critical to effective management of the sales network. These goals typically include sales volume, new customer acquisition, customer satisfaction levels, and individual contribution to team projects. Defining clear and measurable metrics allows you to monitor progress, optimize strategies going forward, and ensure that each team member is aligned with company goals, thereby incentivizing the achievement of tangible results and continuous performance improvement.

### REGULAR MONITORING SYSTEM

Implement a system for regular performance monitoring, which can be supported by CRM software to track sales, customer feedback, and other relevant KPIs.

---

[18] *By purchasing my second book "Managing Your Sales Network," you can download the free bonus " The 16 Essential KPIs to Optimize Your Sales Network." It is a detailed description of the metrics used by sales networks and t h e  calculation system (formulas and examples)*

Schedule regular meetings between vendors and managers to discuss progress, celebrate successes, and address challenges.

### CONSTRUCTIVE AND PERSONALIZED FEEDBACK
Provide constructive feedback, emphasizing positive aspects of performance and identifying opportunities for growth in a specific and pragmatic way. Use concrete examples and data to support feedback, making it as objective and useful as possible.

### INDIVIDUALIZED DEVELOPMENT PLANS
Develop individualized action plans based on performance monitoring results, which may include additional training, mentoring, or special projects to develop specific skills. Include short- and long-term goals with interim milestones to assess progress.

### ENCOURAGEMENT FOR PERSONAL REFLECTION
Stimulate salespeople to reflect on their own performance and goals, promoting self-assessment as part of their professional development. Provide tools and resources to support self-study and personal growth.

## Periodic Evaluations

### FORMAL
Organize formal performance evaluations on an annual or semiannual basis to discuss results, recognize achievements, and update development plans.

### INFORMAL
Encourage informal and regular feedback meetings to keep the lines of communication open and address any problems or opportunities promptly.

## Regular Sessions

### OBJECTIVES OF THE SESSIONS
Provide vendors with timely and constructive evaluations of their performance. Create an environment of open communication that encourages professional and personal growth. Proactively identify and resolve challenges encountered by salespeople in their daily work.

## STRUCTURING OF THE SESSIONS

### Scheduling and Frequency

Establish a regular cadence for feedback sessions, which could be monthly, quarterly or semi-annually, depending on the organization's needs and individual preferences.

Ensure that sessions are planned in advance and that both manager and vendor are prepared with specific data and observations.

### Pre-Session Preparation

Encourage both managers and salespeople to prepare for feedback sessions by collecting performance data, specific examples of successes and challenges, and personal reflections on their own experiences. Draw up an agenda for the session that includes specific points for discussion, ensuring that both parties are aware of the topics to be covered.

### Structure of the Session

Begin with an acknowledgement of the salesperson's successes and progress, emphasizing the positive aspects of his or her performance. Then move on to discuss areas for improvement, providing specific feedback, based on concrete examples, and discussing strategies to address challenges. Conclude by setting clear goals and specific actions for the next period, including both improvement and professional development aspects.

### Constructive comparison

Ensure that feedback sessions are not one-sided, but provide opportunities for vendors to express their opinions, concerns, and ideas for future improvements.

Openly discuss mutual expectations and how the manager can better support the salesperson in achieving his or her goals. In the last chapter this aspect will be discussed in more detail.

### Documentation and Follow-up

Record key points discussed during the session, goals set, and actions agreed upon for future reference.

Schedule follow-ups to monitor progress against established goals and adjust support strategies if necessary.

### *Benefits of Regular Feedback Sessions*
Continuous improvement of individual and sales team performance. Strengthening relationships between managers and salespeople, based on trust and open communication. Early identification of problems and development opportunities, enabling proactive interventions.

## **Customized Development Plans**

### *Objectives of the Plans*
Provide clear and measurable growth paths for salespeople that are aligned with both personal and business goals. Identify and leverage professional development opportunities to strengthen existing skills and acquire new ones.
Encourage salespeople's commitment and motivation through customized and achievable development goals.

### *Initial Assessment of Competencies*
Begin with a comprehensive assessment of the salesperson's current skills and performance, identifying strengths and areas for improvement. Use feedback from previous sessions, performance evaluations, and self-assessments to create a detailed overview.

### *Definition of Development Goals*
As we have already seen, it is necessary to establish specific, measurable, achievable, relevant, and timed (SMART) development goals that address both the individual needs of the salesperson and the strategic goals of the company. Goals may relate to acquiring new technical skills, improving soft skills, or advancing to roles of greater responsibility.

### *Selection of Development Activities*
Identify the most appropriate training and development activities to achieve established goals, which may include training courses, participation in workshops, mentoring sessions, or special projects. Provide for on-the-job learning opportunities, such as assignment to new markets or customer segments, to develop practical skills.

### *Timing and Milestone Scheduling[19]*
Establish a clear timeline for achieving goals, with interim checkpoints to monitor progress.
Ensure that the schedule is realistic and takes into account the daily work responsibilities of the salesperson.

### *Support and Resources*
Determine the support and resources needed to implement the plan, including training budgets, access to training materials, and support from managers or mentors. Establish a system of accountability[20], in which the vendor and manager meet regularly to discuss progress and necessary adjustments to the plan.

### CONTINUOUS EVALUATION AND UPDATING
Implement an ongoing evaluation process to monitor progress toward development goals and to gather feedback on training activities. Update the development plan periodically to reflect changes in business needs, the vendor's professional interests, and progress achieved.

> Setting clear and measurable goals is crucial to the success of any sales strategy. Fair incentive plans, business context analysis, and alignment of goals with corporate missions and visions motivate the team and improve performance. Tailoring goals to reflect individual competencies and territory specificities optimizes sales performance, ensuring sustainable growth aligned with long-term goals.

---

19 *Milestones as intermediate goals*
20 *Accountability system: system of accountability for one's decisions and actions*

# 7. Effective Communication

Effective communication is the backbone of an organization, especially a business network. It goes without saying to remark that interpersonal communication between flesh-and-blood individuals will always be best; but it would be dangerous to snub digital communication tools that enable quick and effective exchanges, such as instant messaging software, CRM systems with collaborative capabilities, and video conferencing platforms. Strategies to facilitate effective communication through the use of communication platforms are crucial in the digital age, especially for sales networks that often operate in dynamic and geographically dispersed environments. Adopting modern digital communication tools can radically transform the way teams interact, collaborate and achieve their goals. On the following pages you will find some of the most popular digital platforms currently in use.

Remember: knowing the management systems that are being used by your team is important so that you can understand whether it is the best fit for your organization and, if appropriate, take action in order to optimize its use by your employees.

# COMMUNICATION IN EVERYDAY LIFE

## Instant Messaging Software

### SLACK
An instant messaging platform that enables the creation of dedicated channels for teams or projects, facilitating real-time communication and collaboration.

### MICROSOFT TEAMS
Integrated with the Microsoft Office 365 productivity suite, Teams offers group chat, video conferencing and document collaboration capabilities.

## CRM Systems with Collaborative Features

### SALESFORCE
One of the most popular CRM systems, Salesforce offers collaborative features through Chatter, an internal social platform that allows team members to share information and collaborate on sales opportunities.

### HUBSPOT CRM
Provides integrated collaboration tools that enable sales teams to manage pipelines, share contacts, and coordinate sales activities.

## Videoconferencing Platforms

### ZOOM
Having become popular for its ease of use and reliability, Zoom supports video conferencing, online meetings and webinars, making it an essential tool for remote communication.

### GOOGLE MEET
Integrated with Google Workspace (formerly G Suite), Google Meet offers a simple solution for video conferencing, accessible directly from Gmail or Google Calendar.

# Project Management and Collaboration Tools

### ASANA
A project management platform that enables teams to coordinate and track the progress of activities, improving transparency and collaboration.

### TRELLO
Based on a Kanban card system, Trello facilitates the organization of projects through cards and lists, making the status of activities visible to all team members.

## Collaborative Platforms

### NOTION
A knowledge management all-rounder that enables the creation of notes, databases, kanban, and collaborative documents, becoming a unified workspace for teams.

### MIRO
A collaborative digital whiteboard platform that supports brainstorming, strategic planning, and visual workshops, facilitating remote creative collaboration.

## Future integration with AI

While these tools are currently among the most popular and useful, it is important to remain open and adaptable to new and emerging technologies. The adoption of artificial intelligence and the integration of advanced data analysis capabilities into CRM systems are examples of how business communication and collaboration may evolve in the future.

# COMMUNICATION IN EDUCATION

The training and Onboarding process, discussed earlier, is also facilitated by digital platforms that allow training paths to be offered to new hires directly from home, eliminating the need for travel. This translates into significant savings in time and money for everyone, especially when the corporate office is located at a great distance.

## **Recommended platforms for onboarding**

### BAMBOOHR
Comprehensive human resource management solution, including a robust onboarding suite. Enables automation of many parts of the onboarding process, from digital signing of documents to introduction to company policies

### WORKDAY
Cloud-based human resource and financial management that includes onboarding capabilities. It is suitable for large organizations seeking an integrated HR and onboarding solution

### LATEX
Platform focused on performance and goal management, which also includes onboarding features. It is particularly useful for setting clear goals and tracking the progress of new employees.

### SLACK
Despite not being a dedicated onboarding platform, Slack facilitates communication and integration of new employees.
Creating dedicated onboarding channels can help new hires feel connected and supported.

Regarding the onboarding phase, we point out previously mentioned applications for communication in general.

*Trello* takes a visual approach to project and task management, setting itself up as a simple yet effective tool in organizing onboarding activities.

*Asana* represents another project management solution that is particularly effective for onboarding. This tool enables the development of specific onboarding projects, characterized by assigned tasks and well-defined deadlines. Its key features include task and subtask management, creation of timelines (time sequences), and the ability to integrate with other applications.

## CONSIDERATIONS FOR CHOICE

When you have to choose the most suitable platform you should ask yourself the following questions:

> *1. Does the platform support the needs of a small startup as well as those of a global organization?*
> *2. Does it easily integrate with other tools already in use (e.g., HR systems, communication tools)?*
> *3. Can the onboarding process be customized to fit the company's specific culture and needs?*
> *4. Is it intuitive for both HR managers and new hires?*

Choosing the right platform will depend on the organization's specific needs and personal preferences. It is advisable to evaluate several options, considering ease of use, scalability and available integrations to find the most suitable solution.

# Integration with Existing Systems

Integrate communication platforms with CRM systems and other business technologies to create a cohesive technology ecosystem and enable vendors to access critical information and communicate in real time.

## COMMUNICATION PROTOCOLS

Establish clear protocols for the use of communication platforms, including times when availability is expected, guidelines on what information to share, and how to handle sensitive or urgent communications.

### PROMOTION OF DISTANCE COLLABORATION
Use video conferencing platforms to hold regular meetings, team brainstorming and training sessions

### MONITORING AND FEEDBACK
Monitor the use and effectiveness of digital communication tools, gathering feedback from vendors

### CONTINUOUS UPDATING AND IMPROVEMENT
Maintain a proactive approach to the use of communication platforms, keeping abreast of the latest technological innovations.

## Benefits of Communication Platforms

### GREATER EFFICIENCY
Real-time communication and immediate access to information reduce waiting time and improve issue resolution.

### FLEXIBILITY
The ability to communicate and collaborate from anywhere gives vendors greater flexibility and supports hybrid or fully remote working models.

### TRANSPARENCY
Facilitated sharing of information and updates through digital platforms contributes to greater transparency within teams and between different business departments.

### TEAM INVOLVEMENT.
Tools such as instant messaging and video conferencing can help maintain active participation by team members, promoting a positive and inclusive corporate culture.

## Regular Meetings

It is recommended to hold regular meetings, both virtual and physical, to discuss progress, challenges and opportunities together with the team. The frequency of meetings should be carefully considered so as not to take valuable time away from the sales force. Therefore, when the meetings are convened, the presence of participants should not be perceived as optional.

## DAILY/ WEEKLY ALIGNMENT
Short (15-30 minutes) to discuss the day's or week's goals, share quick updates, and address any immediate obstacles. Useful for keeping team cohesion high and ensuring that everyone is informed and focused on priorities.

## MONTHLY PERFORMANCE MEETINGS
More detailed meetings to assess monthly progress toward sales goals, analyze performance metrics, and discuss operational strategies. Opportunity to celebrate successes, recognize individual and collective contributions, and recalibrate strategies as needed.

## QUARTERLY OR SEMI-ANNUAL STRATEGY MEETINGS.
Focus on long-term strategic review and planning. These meetings provide an in-depth review of market trends, product performance, and competitive strategies. They are ideal times to review annual goals, adjust sales strategies, and plan future initiatives.

# Maximizing Meetings

## PREPARATION AND AGENDA
Distribute a clear agenda before each meeting, outlining the topics to be discussed, the objectives of the meeting, and the supporting materials needed.
This helps participants prepare properly and contribute more meaningfully.

Let's look at an example.

*WEEKLY EMAIL SALES MEETING*

*EMAIL SUBJECT:* Sales Meeting Agenda

*RECIPIENTS:* Sales Team.

*EMAIL BODY:*

*Dear members of the sales team,*

*To make sure we make the most of our time together in this week's sales meeting, I enclose the agenda and supporting materials needed.*

*Please take time to review the attached items and documents before our meeting so that you can actively contribute to the discussion.*

**Date** *and Time: [Enter date and time].*
*Platform/Location: [Insert details Zoom/link or physical location]*

**Agenda**

<u>Opening (5 minutes)</u>
*Brief welcome and introduction by the sales manager.*

<u>Sales Performance Update (15 minutes)</u>
- *Presentation of the previous week's sales performance against targets.*
- *Supporting materials: Weekly sales report (attached).*

<u>Review of Key Opportunities and Challenges (20 minutes)</u>
- *Guided discussion on recent successes and challenges encountered, with focus on specific cases.*

*Sales Strategies and Best Practices (15 minutes)*
- *Sharing of effective sales strategies and introduction of new techniques or tools.*
- *Supporting materials:*
*Guide to new sales techniques (attached).*

<u>Training and Development (10 minutes)</u>
- *Updates on future training sessions and development opportunities.*
- *Supporting materials:*

> *Calendar of upcoming training sessions (attached).*
>
> <u>*Feedback and Open Questions (10 minutes)*</u>
> *Dedicated space for feedback, questions and proposals from the team.*
>
> <u>*Closing and Next Steps (5 minutes)*</u>
> - *Summary of actions agreed upon during the meeting and definition of next steps.*
> - *Supporting Materials Attached:*
> - *Weekly sales report.pdf*
> - *Summary of opportunities and challenges.docx*
> - *Guide to new sales techniques.pdf*
> - *Training calendar.xlsx*
>
> *I ask that you arrive prepared, having read the materials and ready to share your ideas and feedback. Your active participation is critical to the success of our team.*
>
> *Sincerely,*
> *[Name of Sales Manager]*

This example shows how careful preparation and a clear agenda can guide the structure of a meeting, ensuring that all participants are informed about the topics to be discussed and ready to contribute meaningfully. Sending out supporting materials in advance also helps ensure that the discussion is focused and productive.

## Active Participation

Encourage the active participation of all team members by assigning specific roles (*e.g., moderator, secretary*) and fostering an environment where every opinion is valued.

### EFFECTIVE USE OF TIME

Strictly adhere to set times for the start and end of meetings. Consider using techniques such as the tomato technique[21] for segments of intensive work followed by short breaks.

### FOLLOW-UP AND CONCLUDING ACTIONS
Conclude each meeting with a summary of decisions made, actions to be taken, and responsibilities assigned.
Distribute a recap email or post-meeting minutes to ensure that everyone is aligned and accountable.

### EVALUATION AND FEEDBACK
Periodically, collect feedback on the meetings to evaluate their effectiveness and make improvements. This may include adjusting the frequency of meetings, formats, or content discussed.

## UPDATES AND NEWSLETTERS

Regular distribution of internal updates and newsletters is strategic for keeping the sales team informed, engaged and motivated. It also helps to strengthen corporate culture, promote transparency and stimulate collaboration.

## Creation

### IDENTIFICATION OF CONTENT
Define the types of content that will be most useful and interesting to the sales team. This may include product updates, sales successes, upcoming marketing strategies, employee recognition, and customer success stories.

### SCHEDULING AND FREQUENCY
Establish a regular cadence for publishing updates and newsletters. The frequency can vary from weekly to monthly, depending on the information needs of the team and the dynamism of the industry.

---

21 The *tomato technique* is a time management method developed by Francesco Cirillo in the 1980s. It takes its name from a tomato-shaped kitchen timer, but can be used with any timer. The technique is based on a fractional work approach of dividing time into manageable blocks, usually 25 minutes long, called "tomatoes." Each tomato is followed by a short rest break, usually 5 minutes, before starting a new tomato.

## Format and Design
Develop a visually appealing and easily navigable format for updates and newsletters.
Use images, icons and layouts that facilitate reading and capture readers' interest.

## Distribution Platforms
Select the most effective and universally accessible platforms that may include e-mail, corporate intranet, or knowledge management platforms.

## Team Involvement.
Encourage sales team members to contribute ideas for content, success stories, or suggestions. This not only enriches the published material but also promotes a sense of ownership and value within the team.

## Measuring Impact
Use analytical tools to track opening, reading, and interaction with updates and newsletters.

# **Benefits**

## Team Alignment
Keep all members of the sales team aligned on business strategies, goals, and news.

## Recognition and Motivation
Celebrating successes and recognizing individual and team contributions can significantly increase motivation.

## Knowledge Sharing
Facilitating the exchange of information, tricks of the trade and lessons learned promotes continuous learning and innovation.

## Corporate Cohesion
Strengthening the sense of belonging and building a positive and inclusive corporate culture.

We have just seen about how 'adopting effective communication tools and holding strategy meetings are essential for onboarding. Regular newsletters and updates keep new hires informed and engaged, promoting transparency and corporate ownership.

Integrating existing communication systems ensures a constant flow of information, improving collaboration and efficiency. Using communication platforms facilitates productive meetings with clear objectives. Continuous, well-structured communication is critical for quick and effective onboarding, contributing to sales goals and professional growth of the team.

# 8. Support Strategies

Provide access to continuing education programs to develop sales skills, product knowledge, and technology skills. Consider using e- learning platforms to facilitate autonomous and flexible learning. Providing Continuing Education and Development to salespeople is vital to keep pace with rapidly changing market dynamics, technological advances and increasing customer expectations. Implementing a continuing education program helps develop advanced sales skills, deepen product knowledge, and improve technological effectiveness.

## CONTINUING EDUCATION PROGRAMS

### ASSESSMENT OF TRAINING NEEDS
Begin with an analysis of existing skills and training gaps within the sales team. This can be done through performance evaluations, surveys, and direct feedback from salespeople.

### CUSTOMIZATION OF PATHWAYS
Develop customized learning paths that reflect the individual needs of salespeople, their areas of interest, and their career goals. This personalized approach increases the engagement and effectiveness of training.

# Leveraging E-learning Platforms.

They offer flexibility in terms of time and location, allowing vendors to learn at their own pace. It is possible to select platforms that support a variety of learning formats, such as videos, texts, interactive quizzes, and simulations. Some recommended e-learning platforms that support a variety of learning formats and are ideal for salesperson training:

## LINKEDIN LEARNING

It offers a wide range of courses in areas such as sales, marketing, soft skills, use of specific software, and more. Courses are presented in video formats and often include accompanying materials, quizzes and certificates of completion. LinkedIn Learning is integrated with one of the largest professional networks in the world, making it a valuable resource for marketers seeking to expand their skills and professional connections.

## COURSERA

It partners with universities and organizations around the world to offer online courses on various topics, including sales and marketing strategies. Coursera offers courses designed by top educational institutions and leading companies, ensuring high quality and internationally recognized content.

## UDEMY

A wide selection of courses on topics ranging from sales and negotiation techniques to the use of CRM and data analysis tools. Formats include videos, articles and downloadable resources. Udemy offers the flexibility of access to an extensive library of sales-specific courses, with salespeople able to select those that best suit their learning needs.

## HUBSPOT ACADEMY

Specializing in marketing, sales and related services, this platform offers free courses, video tutorials and tests. It is especially useful for learning the effective use of CRM systems and inbound marketing strategies. It is ideal for marketers who wish to deepen their knowledge in digital marketing and the use of HubSpot's CRM, with industry-recognized certifications.

## SKILLSHARE

Focused on sharing creative and professional skills through hands-on projects and video lessons. Includes courses on topics such as effective communication, time management, and sales techniques. Skillshare promotes a hands-on approach to learning, ideal for salespeople seeking to improve their soft skills in an interactive way.

## **Continuing Product Education**

Ensure that salespeople receive regular updates and training on the latest product innovations, features, and benefits.

### SOFT SKILLS DEVELOPMENT

Integrate into continuing education modules dedicated to the development of soft skills, such as negotiation, effective communication, time management and conflict resolution.
These skills are crucial to success in the sales role.

### CERTIFICATIONS AND PATHWAYS TO GROWTH

Provide opportunities to obtain professional certifications or attend external workshops and industry conferences.
This not only enriches training but also contributes to the professional growth of salespeople.

*EXAMPLE COMMUNICATION OF PATHWAY OF GROWTH AND CERTIFICATION OPPORTUNITIES*

> *BUSINESS CONTEXT*
> *A software company that specializes in business intelligence solutions wants to enhance the skills of its sales team by keeping staff up-to-date on the latest technology and sales practices in the tech industry.*

## TEXT ANNOUNCEMENT

Subject: New Growth and Certification Opportunities for the Sales Team!

## MESSAGE BODY

Dear members of the sales team,
We are excited to announce the launch of our new professional growth program, designed to support your professional development and strengthen our overall sales capabilities.

Here are the opportunities available:
1) **Certification in business intelligence and data analysis**
Description:
An online certificate program offered by [Institute Name], a leader in the field of data analytics. This course will provide you with an in-depth understanding of the latest technologies and practices in business intelligence,

Benefits:
Improve the ability to communicate the value of our solutions to customers with a solid understanding of the principles of data analysis.

How to Enroll:
Send your request to [Email HR/Training Manager] by [Date].

2) **Workshop on advanced sales techniques**
Description: A two-day workshop, taught by a well-known expert in the tech sales industry, focusing on advanced negotiation and closing strategies.

Benefits:
Acquire new techniques and strategies to improve sales performance and overcome customer objections.

DATE AND PLACE: *[Insert details]*,

How to Participate:
Reserve your place through the link provided on [Internal Platform].

### 3) Participation in industry conferences
Description:
Annual opportunities to attend relevant conferences in B.I. and technology, [Conference Name].

Benefits:
Networking with industry professionals, learning about the latest trends and innovations, and representing our company in the industry.

Mode of Selection:
Submit a brief proposal on how attending the conference will benefit your professional development and our company to [Email HR/Training Manager].

Corporate Support
The company will cover registration costs and, for conferences, travel and lodging expenses. In addition, participants in the certificate program will receive a bonus upon successful completion of the course.

Why Participate.
These opportunities will not only enrich your professional experience but also contribute significantly to our corporate mission. We are committed to your development and the success of our sales team.
For any questions or further information, please feel free to contact

[Name of Person Responsible].

Sincerely,

[Your Name][Location][Company]

# Evaluation of the Impact of Training

### FEEDBACK AND EVALUATION
Collect regular feedback from participants to evaluate the effectiveness of training programs and make improvements where necessary.

### PERFORMANCE MONITORING
Monitor sales performance before and after training to assess the tangible impact of development programs on productivity and sales.

## Mentoring and Coaching
As covered earlier in previous chapters we still recall how critical it is to implement mentoring and coaching programs, matching experienced salespeople with new hires or salespeople who need additional support.

This contributes to professional development and strengthens the supportive culture within the team.

# SALES RESOURCES AND MARKETING MATERIALS

Easy access to up-to-date sales resources, marketing materials, and presentation tools is critical to enable salespeople to effectively communicate the value of the products or services they offer and to successfully navigate the sales process. The availability of quality materials is basic to supporting sales efforts. These tools not only support sales efforts but also help build and maintain a cohesive brand narrative.

Let's see what characteristics they must have.

# Access to Resources

## CENTRALIZATION OF RESOURCES
Create a centralized digital library where salespeople can easily access all necessary sales and marketing materials. This can include brochures, presentations, case studies, product fact sheets, videos, and customer testimonials.

## EASE OF ACCESS
Use platforms that allow easy access from mobile and desktop devices, ensuring that vendors can access resources wherever they are, whether in the office or in the field.

## BRAND CONSISTENCY
Brand consistency is crucial for any company. It is important that all promotional materials, communications, and customer interactions faithfully reflect the company's branding and messages. Maintaining this consistency strengthens brand reputation and increases customer trust, facilitating long-term brand recognition and loyalty.

# Resource Use Training

## SPECIFIC TRAINING
Provide specific training on the most effective ways to use sales and marketing materials during the sales cycle.
This may include workshops on how to customize presentations for specific clients or industries.

## DYNAMIC PRESENTATION TOOLS
Investing in tools that enable salespeople to create dynamic, interactive presentations that can adapt to customers' specific needs and interests during sales meetings is essential. Using tablets or PCs to update resources makes the process less expensive than traditional printing. This not only reduces operational costs but also promotes greater flexibility and environmental sustainability by allowing updates to be distributed in

efficiently and without wasting paper, should you decide not to print.

### FEEDBACK AND CONTINUOUS IMPROVEMENT
Encourage vendors to provide feedback on available sales and marketing materials, including information on what is working well and what could be improved.

## Benefits of Accessing Sales Resources

### IMPROVING EFFICIENCY
Having pre-packaged and easily customizable materials available reduces the time salespeople have to spend preparing presentations, allowing them to focus on selling.

### GREATER SALES EFFECTIVENESS
Well-designed and informative materials can help communicate the value of products or services more convincingly, increasing the chances of closing sales.

### CONSISTENCY OF MESSAGE
Standardized materials ensure that all salespeople convey cohesive and accurate messages about the company's products, services, and values.

### CUSTOMER SATISFACTION
Providing customers with clear, professional and easily understandable information improves their overall experience and can strengthen their trust in the brand.

# OPERATIONAL AND ADMINISTRATIVE SUPPORT

An often overlooked but crucial detail is the reduction of salespeople's workload related to tasks unrelated to selling. Such a strategy allows salespeople to focus more intensely on truly fruitful actions, such as interacting with customers and closing deals. This means completing sales, finalizing deals, and ensuring that transactions are successfully completed. In this way, it elevates the efficiency and job satisfaction of salespeople Implementing smooth communication between different business sectors is equally vital, ensuring that the needs of one department are understood and welcomed by others. For example, during the induction period, I suggest that the new employee spend a little time with the administrative team, promoting a mutual understanding of business functions. If feasible, holding reverse sessions, where staff from other areas experience the daily grind of sales, can further enrich this interchange of perspectives.

## PROCESS AUTOMATION
Invest in tools and software that automate sales and administrative processes, such as order management, updating customer databases, and sales reporting. This can include CRM systems that facilitate customer relationship management and data collection.

## VIRTUAL OR PHYSICAL ASSISTANCE
Provide salespeople with access to virtual or physical assistants who can take care of administrative tasks, such as scheduling appointments, preparing necessary sales documentation, and managing emails.

## TRAINING ON THE USE OF TOOLS
Ensure that salespeople receive adequate training in the use of automation and management tools.

## INTERNAL SUPPORT CENTERS
Establish internal support centers or contact persons to whom vendors can turn for any clarification.

## WORKFLOW OPTIMIZATION
Regularly reviewing and optimizing workflows and administrative processes is critical to identify any inefficiencies or bottlenecks that may be slowing down vendors. So that they can focus on their core activities without being burdened by cumbersome procedures or delays.

### Delegation of Non-Essential Tasks
Encourage salespeople to delegate nonessential tasks that do not require their specific expertise in sales. Although this may need a cultural change for some, it is a decisive factor in getting employees used to optimizing the use of their time.

### Opinion Gathering and Continuous Improvement
Regularly collect opinions from vendors on the type and quality of support offered. Use these evaluations to implement continuous improvements to the support services provided. In addition, this exchange of perceptions allows support strategies and tools to be refined, making them increasingly in line with the real needs of the sales force.

## Benefits of Administrative Support

### Increased Focus on Sales
By reducing the non-sales workload, salespeople can focus more on sales activities and developing customer relationships.

### Increased Productivity and Efficiency
More time to handle more customers and more sales opportunities . This approach helps to decrease errors and speed up sales cycles, thereby optimizing overall efficiency.

### Improvement of the Satisfaction of Sellers
Reducing the stress associated with handling administrative tasks contributes to the satisfaction and motivation of salespeople.

*This chapter shows how investing in continuing education and flexible learning resources is essential to keeping salespeople competitive. Customized pathways and e-learning platforms enrich skills and strengthen team performance. Development tools and programs, with needs assessment and* continuous updating on products and soft skills, contribute significantly to professional growth and successful sales strategies.

# 9. Recognition and Incentives

The application of recognition and incentive systems is the most important critical factor in motivating salespeople, valuing both their individual and team contributions. A well-designed system not only stimulates sales performance, but also reinforces the sense of belonging and positive corporate culture that we know are indispensable to the achievement of any sales team's performance.

## DEFINITION OF CLEAR CRITERIA

Establish clear and transparent criteria for recognition and incentives. These criteria should be directly linked to business and sales objectives, ensuring that salespeople know exactly what is required to achieve recognition.

## VARIETY OF INCENTIVES

Create an incentive system that includes a variety of rewards, both monetary and nonmonetary. This can include bonuses, extra commissions, award trips, public recognition, exclusive training opportunities, and more.

## PUBLIC RECOGNITION

Public recognition in the corporate environment is a powerful motivational lever that goes beyond mere appreciation staff, playing a crucial role in social approval among colleagues. This kind of recognition not only validates individual or team achievements but also helps build a positive corporate culture based on recognition of merit and encouragement of performance.

## Strategies for Public Recognition

### CORPORATE MEETINGS
Use company meetings as an opportunity to announce the successes of salespeople or sales teams. These moments can range from small milestones to major accomplishments, such as exceeding sales goals or successfully launching a difficult campaign.

### SUCCESS STORIES
Publishing success stories, vendor recognition, and milestones in, for example, the House organ or internal newsletter is an effective strategy. This not only gives visibility to outstanding vendors, but also serves as a powerful motivational tool for the entire staff. Showcasing these successes helps create a positive and inspiring work environment, encouraging all team members to aim for excellence and celebrate achievements, thereby strengthening internal cohesion and commitment to company goals.

### INTERNAL COMMUNICATION PLATFORMS
Use corporate intranet platforms or simply whtsapp or Telegram groups to share successes in real time. Creating dedicated recognition channels can encourage other colleagues to offer kudos and support.

### FORMAL RECOGNITION PROGRAMS
Establish formal recognition programs, such as "Vendor of the Month" or "Team of the Year," with clear and transparent criteria. These programs can include tangible rewards in addition to public recognition.

### AWARDS CEREMONIES
Organize annual or semi-annual events dedicated to the celebration of outstanding performance. These ceremonies, to be held in exquisite or special settings at venues outside the company,

may include award ceremonies, leadership recognition speeches, and networking moments.

## Benefits of Public Recognition

### MOTIVATION AND ENGAGEMENT

Public recognition increases salespeople's motivation and improves their engagement, leading to higher productivity and job satisfaction.

### POSITIVE CULTURE

It reinforces a corporate culture that values and celebrates success, encouraging a positive, results-oriented mindset.

### SOCIAL APPROVAL

Encourages social approval among colleagues, strengthening interpersonal relationships and promoting a supportive and collaborative work environment.

### CORPORATE ATTRACTIVENESS

Companies that practice public recognition are often seen as desirable employers, helping to attract in recruitment (candidates also do their own investigations) and especially retain our top talent.

## Considerations for Implementation

### EQUITY AND TRANSPARENCY

Ensure that the recognition process is perceived as fair and transparent, with well-defined criteria to avoid perceptions of favoritism. This reinforces employees' confidence in the evaluation system and leadership, further motivating the team toward excellence.

### CUSTOMIZATION

Personalizing the recognition of salespeople's achievements within and outside the organization is a most important practice. By tailoring recognition to the specific achievements and personal characteristics of each salesperson, the value of the recognition itself is increased. This personalization not only increases the visibility of deserving individuals, but also creates an atmosphere of genuine appreciation within the company. Result: a greater motivational impact, inspiring all team members to excel and share their successes, promoting a cohesive company culture geared toward achieving shared goals.

### INCLUSIVENESS
Seek to recognize a variety of contributions, not just higher sales, but also significant improvements, excellence in customer service, or innovative contributions.

Implementing an effective public recognition system requires a well-thought-out approach. When done correctly, public recognition not only celebrates successes but plays a key role in building a strong, motivated and cohesive corporate culture.

## INCENTIVE STRATEGIES

In the effective management of a sales network, the implementation of a well-structured incentive system is key to motivating salespeople and pushing them to meet and exceed set goals. An effective incentive system not only improves individual performance, but also contributes significantly to the overall success of the company.

## Types of Incentives

Incentives can be divided into two main categories: monetary and nonmonetary. Monetary incentives include bonuses, extra commissions, and profit sharing, which are directly related to sales results or the achievement of specific company goals. These financial incentives are often the most direct and tangible for salespeople. In parallel, nonmonetary incentives are becoming increasingly important. These can include public recognition, professional training opportunities, access to exclusive courses, rewards such as unique trips or experiences, and internal promotions. Such incentives tend to build a deeper bond between salespeople and the company, promoting a positive corporate culture and increased brand loyalty.

## **Alignment with Corporate Goals**

To maximize the effectiveness of incentives, it is crucial that they are closely aligned with the company's strategic goals. This means that the criteria for earning incentives should be clear, measurable, achievable, relevant and time-defined (SMART). An effective incentive system should be flexible enough to adapt to market dynamics and individual performance, ensuring that salespeople are always motivated to pursue goals that support the company's overall vision.

## **Evaluation Criteria and Data Analysis**

A critical aspect of incentive management is the performance appraisal system. It is imperative that salespeople receive regular, constructive feedback on their progress against established goals. This not only helps to keep motivation high, but also provides opportunities for continuous improvement and goal adjustment. Feedback sessions should complement incentives by providing a clear picture of performance and areas for improvement.

> Recognition and incentive strategy is a crucial lever for any company's success. Through the application of a well-structured system that values both individual and team achievements, organizations not only stimulate sales performance but also fortify internal cohesion and corporate culture. By combining tangible recognition and development opportunities, dynamic work environments are created where salespeople are constantly motivated to excel and actively contribute to shared corporate goals.

# 10. Two-way Communication

Two-way communication is not limited to a simple top-down exchange of information, but encourages an open and ongoing dialogue where salespeople are actively involved in sharing feedback, successes, and challenges. Fostering a corporate culture that values two-way communication can transform the way an organization responds to the needs of its customers, adapts to market changes, and innovates its processes.

## FREEDOM TO EXPRESS ONESELF

Two-way communication increases transparency within the organization. Salespeople who feel they can freely express their opinions and share their experiences contribute to an open and honest work environment. Such an environment-always with respect for roles and in the correct forms-generates a number of benefits and reduces negativity.

### INCREASED EMPLOYEE ENGAGEMENT.
Feeling heard and having the opportunity to influence business decisions increases salesperson engagement and satisfaction. This, in turn, can lead to higher productivity and lower turnover.

### EARLY IDENTIFICATION OF CHALLENGES AND OPPORTUNITIES.
Two-way communication enables business leaders to quickly identify and address challenges, as well as capitalize on emerging opportunities, with information gathered directly from the sales force.

### CONTINUOUS IMPROVEMENT
Feedback gathered through two-way communication can be used to continuously improve processes, products and sales strategies, keeping the company competitive and on the cutting edge.

### COMMUNICATION TOOLS AND PLATFORMS
Provide tools and platforms that facilitate two-way communication, such as internal forums, instant messaging systems, and feedback management platforms.

### REGULAR MEETINGS AND LISTENING SESSIONS
Hold regular meetings and dedicated listening sessions where salespeople can share their ideas, feedback and concerns directly with management.

### OPEN DOOR POLICIES
Adopt an open-door policy, encouraging salespeople to feel free to approach their superiors with ideas or concerns at any time.

### EFFECTIVE COMMUNICATION TRAINING
Provide training on how to communicate effectively, including courses on active listening, constructive expression of feedback, and conflict resolution techniques.

### ACKNOWLEDGMENT OF CONTRIBUTION
Recognize and value the contributions of vendors, both publicly and privately, to show the company's appreciation for their efforts and ideas.

---

#### EXAMPLE 1: TEAM MEETING IN PRESENCE.

*Context:*
*Monthly team meeting where progress, goals and challenges are discussed.*

*Dialogue Simulation:*
Manager: "Good morning everyone, thank you for being here. Before we start with today's agenda, I would like to hear from each of you. What were the biggest challenges you faced this month and how can we work together to overcome them?"
Vendor 1: "Thank you, I have encountered some difficulties in engaging new customers in Sector X. I think we could benefit from more targeted marketing materials."
Manager: "Good point. After the meeting, let's form a small working group to develop these materials.
Any other experiences or suggestions?"
Salesperson 2: "Yes, I noticed that our CRM could be optimized to better track customer interactions. Perhaps we can explore some additional updates or training?"
Manager: "Absolutely, we will look into this possibility. Thank you for the feedback. It is critical for us to continuously improve."

EXAMPLE 2: ONLINE CORPORATE FORUM

*Context:*
An online business forum where vendors can post ideas, challenges and successes.

*Forum posts from a Vendor:*
Title: New Strategies for the Y Market
Message: "Hello everyone, I have had great success by taking a different approach in the Y market. I have customized the presentation of our products to better meet the specific needs of customers in that area. Would it be helpful to share this strategy with the team?"
Manager's response, "Fantastic job! It would be very helpful if you could present your approach in the next company webinar. This type of strategy sharing of success is exactly what we encourage. Thank you for taking the initiative."

*Example 3: Virtual Listening Session.*

**Context:**
*A virtual listening session organized via video conference, dedicated to gathering feedback and ideas.*

**Dialogue Simulation:**
Manager: *"Welcome to this listening session. Today's goal is to better understand your needs and how we can support you. Please feel free to share openly."* Vendor 3: *"I appreciate this opportunity. I think we would need more after-sales support to ensure customer satisfaction. Some customers have expressed a desire for more in-depth product training after purchase."*
Manager: *"This is very important feedback. We will work on a plan to implement after-sales training sessions.*
*Any other ideas or concerns you want to share?"*

# COMPLAINTS AND NEGATIVE FEEDBACK

Managing communication effectively, particularly when it comes to complaints or negative feedback from sales accounts, is a crucial skill for every manager. Turning these situations into positive opportunities requires a strategic and empathetic approach.

## ACTIVE LISTENING

First, it is critical to actively listen to what the sales account is saying, without interruption. Showing that you are paying attention and that you understand their concern can in itself reduce tension.

## Validation of Feelings
Acknowledge and validate the salesperson's feelings, even in situations where their complaints may seem specious. Expressing understanding with phrases such as "*I understand why this might be frustrating for you*" shows empathy. This helps build a relationship of trust and support, showing salespeople that their feelings and perceptions are acknowledged and taken seriously.

## Solutions-Based Approach
Instead of focusing exclusively on the problem, and often on the discomfort the employee is feeling, shift the focus of the conversation to how to find a solution. Asking the salesperson what changes or solutions they would see as helpful can help turn the complaint into a constructive opportunity.

## Encouragement of Personal Responsibility
Help salespeople see how they can play an active role in solving the problem or improving the situation. This encourages personal responsibility and reduces the tendency to complain without taking action. For example, shifting the focus to exogenous obstacles can help the employee focus on actions that are solely up to him or her: a greater understanding of customer needs, one's own approach, follow- up timing, etc.

## Setting Clear Expectations
Often, complaints arise from unmet or misunderstood expectations. Making sure salespeople know what to expect in terms of support, processes, and goals can prevent many complaints. This advance clarification helps to establish clear guidelines and reduce misunderstandings by getting everyone on the same page from the start.

## Positive Communication
Actively seek to share successes, progress, and positive feedback. Creating an environment where successes are celebrated can

help balance the most difficult conversations and build a positive culture.

## CREATING AN OPEN ENVIRONMENT

Fostering a work environment where everyone's opinions are welcome and encourages salespeople to express their fears openly, reducing the risk of unspoken grievances that can erupt later.

> *EXAMPLE: COMPLAINT MANAGEMENT DIALOGUE*
>
> *Manager:*
> *"I noticed that you are concerned about the current situation. I understand your concerns and am grateful that you have shared them with me. Would you like to explore together how to improve things? What solutions might be effective?*
> *How can I offer you the best support in this circumstance?"*

## FOLLOWING THE CASE IN ITS SUBSEQUENT STAGES

After discussing the grievance and agreeing on actions to be taken, it is critical to conduct a follow-up. This process not only demonstrates that the manager seriously evaluates the vendor's concerns, but also evidences a real commitment to the well-being and success of the staff. Carrying out a follow-up reinforces team trust and communication, which is vital to maintaining a positive and productive work environment.

> Finally, in this last chapter, we learned how attentive listening, empathy and collaboration enable managers to solve problems and strengthen trust in sales teams. This promotes a harmonious and productive work environment where salespeople feel heard, valued and supported.

# Conclusion

Developing an effective sales network requires a deep understanding of organizational structures, territorial breakdown, and the careful selection of candidates. From the salesperson to the sales manager, each role plays a key part in achieving company goals.

Ongoing training, clear and measurable goal setting, and effective communication are the key elements in keeping the sales team motivated and aligned. In addition, recognition and incentives are powerful tools for rewarding excellent performance and stimulating continuous improvement.

Remember, the success of your sales network depends on your ability to support and develop each team member by providing the resources and materials needed to excel.

Implement the strategies discussed in this book and you will see your team and your business grow.

*Good work!*

# Exclusive Bonus
## for Readers!

Complimentary for you:
**"Guide for the Selector of New Sales Accounts."**
This guide, an integral part of the book "Building Your Sales Network," is an invaluable aid for those who want to build an effective and successful sales network. It will provide you with practical advice and proven strategies on how to carry out a winning selection process, ensuring that every member of your team contributes the most to sales.

**DON'T MISS THIS UNIQUE OPPORTUNITY TO ELEVATE YOUR SKILLS AND LEAD YOUR BUSINESS TO SUCCESS!**

### How to Access Your Bonus:
1. **Scan the QR Code below** with your smartphone or tablet camera.
2. The link to the exclusive PDF is automatically opened.
3. **Save or view the PDF** to always have at your fingertips the key strategies and practical tips that will transform your approach to sales.

www.ingramcontent.com/pod-product-compliance
Lightning Source LLC
Chambersburg PA
CBHW071102240526
45471CB00016B/2307